Adolf Loos

Panayotis Tournikiotis

Princeton Architectural Press

Published by
Princeton Architectural Press
37 East 7th Street
New York, New York 10003

For a free catalog of books, call toll free 1.800.722.6657 or visit www.papress.com

Original texts and photographic materials
© 1991 Éditions Macula, Paris
Authorized translation from the French language edition
published by Éditions Macula

Printed and bound in Canada

Editing and production: Allison Saltzman
Translation from the French: Marguerite McGoldrick
Special thanks to: Nettie Aljian, Ann Alter, Amanda Atkins, Nicola Bednarek, Janet Behning,
Megan Carey, Penny Chu, Jan Cigliano, Clare Jacobson, Mark Lamster, Nancy Eklund Later,
Linda Lee, Jane Sheinman, Lottchen Shivers, Katharine Smalley, Scott Tennent, Jennifer
Thompson, and Deb Wood of Princeton Architectural Press—Kevin C. Lippert, publisher

The Library of Congress has cataloged the hardcover edition of this book as:
Tournikiotis, Panayotis, 1955–
       [Loos. English]
    Adolf Loos / Panayotis Tournikiotis.
          p.   cm.
    Includes bibliographical references and index.
       1. Loos, Adolf, 1870–1933—Criticism and interpretation.
    2. Functionalism (Architecture)   I. Title.
    NA1011.5.L6T6813   1994
    720'.92—dc20   94–21141
                                                       CIP

ISBN 1-56898-342-5

Adolf Loos

CONTENTS

For Catherine

*I would like to express my thanks to everyone—
researchers, friends and colleagues—
who contributed to this monograph. Especially
Dimitri Philippidés, Jean Péponis and Robert
Trevisiol, for reading the manuscript and for their
suggestions; Rudolf Altmüller, Cultural Consul
of Austria in Paris and Michel Guérin, Cultural
Consul of France in Vienna; Walter Koschatzky,
director of the Graphische Sammlung Albertina,
Vienna; Burkhardt Rukschcio and Hermann
Czech, for their cooperation; and finally,
Pauline Choay, for her successful editing of a
difficult manuscript.*

1   ADOLF LOOS.
Photo by W. Wels, 1912.

CHAPTER ONE
THE ARCHITECT'S ITINERARY

Adolf Loos appears, at first, to be an ambiguous, contradictory and even enigmatic personality, to quote Pevsner.[1] Was he a rationalist, a traditionalist, or indeed a "classicist"? Was he among the pioneers of modern architecture, was he a Dadaist architect, or was he the last breath of a decadent Art Nouveau? Did he follow the principles of the Chicago School, did he prefer Le Corbusier, Gropius, and the other moderns, or was he simply the first post-modern architect? The one-sided, linear histories of architecture (from Morris to Gropius) that trace the path of the Modern Movement raise such questions, but then leave them unanswered. They present Loos's writings, especially "Ornament and Crime," as anti-historicist manifestoes of the era between the two world wars.

Loos's field of critical thought encompassed the whole of Viennese daily life. The moralistic and largely therapeutic thinking reclaimed truth in all its purity, supporting neither lies, nor imitation, nor trompe l'oeil. However, viewing Loos solely as an avant-garde of the twentieth century would miss the richness of his personality, and would deny the particulars that separated him from his supposed successors. Loos always situated himself dialectically to the historic continuity of tradition: he took care to speak of concrete time and space, he opposed the quest for new forms as a refute of history, and more importantly, he criticized the privileged status of the architect as creator and genius.

Adolf Franz Karl Viktor Maria Loos was born on December 10, 1870 in Brünn (known today as Brno), the commercial and industrial center of the Austro-Hungarian Empire, 100 kilometers north of Vienna. His father, who had studied painting and sculpture, was a sculptor and stone cutter; several authors have attributed Loos's preference for beautiful, well-worked materials to his father's trade. But because the father died in 1879, the relationship between his craft and his son's taste for precious materials, was, it seems, more of a psychological order, and could be seen as a type of mourning. Loos began his studies in Brünn; in 1884 he entered the *Obergymnasium* of the Benedictines of Melk, but left almost immediately, after failing the February exams. He then enrolled at the National School of Arts and Crafts in Reichenberg, to become a mechanic. He left once again to enter a program in building technology, and ended with yet another in mechanical construction in 1889 at the National School of Arts and Crafts back in Brünn. He decided then to turn to architecture; he studied at the Superior Technical School in Dresden for two semesters and, after doing his military service, settled in Vienna to take courses at the Academy of Beaux Arts. He then returned to Dresden in 1892, and tried—unsuccessfully—to finish the program he had started three years earlier.

Loos's studies were mediocre. However, his apprenticeship in the technical and construction sections of Arts and Crafts schools gave him experience uncommon among beaux-arts architects. He was able to communicate with the craftsman and the mason, and understand and value the quality of their traditional work. Testimonials present him as one at ease at the building site, although his drawings and sketches were elementary, even rudimentary. Loos, who groped his way along, eventually profited from his disjointed journey.

Loos was one of the first European architects to undertake a trip to the new world after finishing his studies, rather than the traditional grand tour of Italy and Greece. In 1893, he visited the Chicago World's Fair which paid homage to Louis Sullivan—even in the middle of an era of triumphant eclecticism. He then lived in New York where he took on several temporary jobs, and in 1896, left to settle in Vienna. This trip played a very important role in Loos's life; his American experience helped to define his criticism of concurrent European culture, politics, and architecture. It is otherwise difficult to explain his choice to travel to the United States. Doubtless, Loos felt suffocated in the confined and conservative atmosphere of the declining Austro-Hungarian empire, and he thought that in America he would discover realism and freedom, a land where everything was possible. This former student of the Arts and Crafts who had wanted to become a mechanic was probably seduced by the American myth of practicality and hard work. For Loos, this combination symbolized the *esprit* necessary to human progress. It is equally difficult, however, to determine precisely the American influence in his work. In his youth, Loos was impressed by the first skyscrapers, by domestic architecture, and in general, by a society full of vitality that was supported by egalitarian and utilitarian aspirations. He discovered the classical spirit of the engineer—the Greek of modern times—who professed the fusion of beauty and utility in everyday objects. Though he never met Adler or Sullivan, his memory was indelibly marked by the Chicago School, which existed simultaneously with the Greek revival that for half a century—since the end of the 1820s—had dominated monumental architecture in the United States.[2]

Upon returning to Europe, Loos started to work and to write articles and critiques so polemic and insistent that after several years no one in Vienna could ignore their author's existence. Loos wrote of a turn-of-the-century Vienna, one he saw as full of despair and debilitation. Others, like Robert Musil, thought that the elder Viennese, at the end of the century, had awakened the young: "It was a time of great ethical and aesthetic activity. We believed in the future, a social future and a new art. We gave the impression of morbidity and decadence: but these two negative determinants were only the occasional expression of a desire to be different and to act differently from the man of the past. We believed in the future, we wanted to master it."[3]

Was this a value crisis, decadence, an intellectual void? If so, this void was the origin of the creative explosion that made Vienna a place rich in contradictions and ambiguities in

2   ADOLF LOOS.
Drawing by Oskar Kokoschka, 1909.

the first decades of the twentieth century. Art and thought were turned upside-down by those who attempted to formulate a fundamental and essentially positive critique of the modes of accepted expression. The atmosphere created by this crisis of moral and social values and by the questioning of individuality engendered a profound interest in unconscious forces—eros and death—and one saw these themes in all domains. It was the era of the birth of psychoanalysis and Freud, who despite his hate for Vienna, lived there almost all his life because, in spite of everything, it was the most appropriate territory for his research.

The decline in academicism and, simultaneously, the sensualism and decorative obsession of Art Nouveau were noticeably prominent at the beginning of the new century. Kraus, Loos, Schönberg, Wittgenstein, Trakl and Kokoschka intervened with neither precaution nor reserve, and the Empire collapsed in 1918. Though they lived in the same city, united often by friendship despite the diversity of their activities, all these personages remained

3   JOSEPH MARIA OLBRICH (1867–1908): SECESSION BUILDING, VIENNA.
Sketch of entrance, 1896.

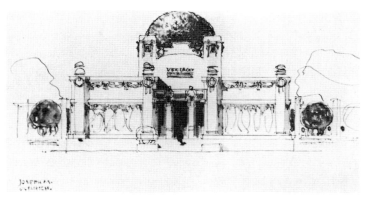

4   JOSEPH MARIA OLBRICH: SECESSION BUILDING, VIENNA.
Sketch of front elevation. Olbrich was a proponent of Viennese Secessionism; Loos severely criticized their work.

independent, without forming groups or writing manifestoes—like "the iron filings of an unmagnetized field."[4] Yet their ideas and projects were bathed in an incontestable unity of tone and inspiration. Their criticisms of society and of culture even went so far as to question language and communication in their most general forms.

It was a question of distilling the necessary from the arbitrary or superfluous components of expression and usage;[5] an attack against the pseudo-sophistication of bourgeois aestheticism and against the unbounded use of the false, which were overwhelmingly considered signs of the generally deceptive nature of society. They set out on a search for "authenticity" and their criticism was characterized by a fusion of the ethical and the aesthetic. Loos believed that a society which, by various deceptions, intended to mask its emptiness and spiritual poverty, was a miserable society. Loos also considered loyalty to out-moded construction and anachronistic ornamentation to be immoral. According to him, functional objects needed no ornamentation. Opposed to all "styles"—and even the notion of style—he conceived his houses based on functional interiors, leaving the facades rigorously simple. As for his public buildings, he professed that they needed "expressive" facades (in the sense of "*l'architecture parlante*," see chapters 4 and 6) which would not tear at the urban fabric. Among Loos's contemporaries, the consensus was to eschew all ornament, as much in philosophy as in art: a predilection for stripped, severe forms, and sobriety and rigor in the choice of means.

Loos began to write in the same year as the creation of the Secession;[6] one finds ideas in his first writings which were adopted and repeated by the avant-garde of the nineteen-twenties. He started with a diagnosis: "But today it is not only by...the furnishings of one's residence (which consist of outright imitations), but also by one's residence itself, the building in which one lives, that everyone wants to make himself out to be something more than he is."[7] The Vienna of his time seemed to him "a Potemkin city,"[8] a city of trompe l'oeil aristocracy: "Supply and demand regulate architectural form....The building speculator would most dearly like to have his facades entirely plastered from top to bottom. It costs the least. And at the same time, he would be acting in the truest, most correct, and most artistic way. But people would not want to move into the building. And so, in the interest of rentability, the landlord is forced to nail on a particular kind of facade, and only this kind. Yes, literally nail on! For these Renaissance and Baroque palaces are not actually made out of the material of which they seem....Their ornamental details, their corbels, festoons, cartouches, and denticulation, are nailed-on poured cement. Of course, this technique too, which comes into use for the first time in this century, is perfectly legitimate. But it does not do to use it with forms whose origin is intimately bound up with a specific material simply because no technical difficulties stand in the way. It would have been the artist's task to find a new formal language for new materials. Everything else is imitation."[9]

In opposing himself vehemently to the masking of materials and to the travesty of ancient decorative practices, from 1898 on Loos announced what was to become one of the major preoccupations of modern architects. He concluded that "materials should be worked in such a way that it is impossible to confuse the clad material with its cladding" (see chapter 3).

Loos did not oppose eclecticism: he took aim at the false-seeming, the act of hiding materiality behind an appearance of truth. He did not challenge historical references in contemporary architecture, merely the false usage common to the age. Faced with the art and architecture of his time, Loos's position is very clear: he rebelled against Art Nouveau, considering it even less adapted to the modern world than imitations of ancient styles. It was at Van de Velde that he directed his most caustic critiques: "There will come a time when detention in a cell managed by the taste...of Professor Van de Velde will be considered an aggravation of pain."[10] Loos spared Olbrich and Hoffmann no less: he accused them of having, under the pretext of style, conquered and corrupted traditional family furniture—which wanted only to stay loyal to its slow, gradual evolution. It was useless, according to Loos, to modify the form of objects already adapted to their function. He altogether admired the Americans and the English—the first for their simplicity, the second for their discretion. He loved the automobile and its formal purity, he praised plumbing for its healthy and fascinating functionality, and electricity for its multiple uses. But he was sensitive only to their utilitarian beauty, to the progress that they had afforded; he did not admire them in so far as the machinery was concerned. He was seduced neither by industry nor technology, both of which he considered fatal to the historic evolution of humanity; he did not expect that they could cure the "illnesses" of his contemporaries, and claimed no part in the founding of a machine-based society. His model was the artisan, the man connected to objects that he has created and produced, in whom truth, distinction, history, and creation were incarnated.

During the decade that followed his return to Europe, Loos was introduced into Vienna's intellectual milieu. He formed close friendships with Karl Kraus, Peter Altenberg and Arnold Schönberg. They frequented literary cafes[11] and took part in discussions and debates (on *Tristan and Isolde*, and on Wagner, who had always impassioned Loos).

Most of Loos's essays and critiques developed from these discussions; he was a strong presence in the cultural life of the city. In 1903 he published two volumes of *Das andere*, "a journal for the introduction of Western civilization in Austria," which he wrote entirely himself. In it he discussed the daily life of his contemporaries, and criticized them relentlessly. As a participant in most of the city's artistic events, he arduously defended endeavors at new expressions against the distrust or hostility of the public. He was often seen at the concerts of Schönberg or those of Schönberg's students: He was at the March 31, 1913 premier of Berg's *Altenberg Lieder* that the police disrupted.[12] At the first Exposition of

5   OTTO WAGNER (1841–1918):
     VILLA WAGNER, VIENNA.
     Perspective, 1905.

6   OTTO WAGNER: APARTMENT HOUSE, VIENNA.
     Perspective, 1909. Adolf Loos admired Wagner,
     who knew how to "forget that he was an
     architect, and slip into the skin of the craftsman."

Arts held in Vienna he acquired *Guerrier*, an extremely controversial work by the young expressionist Oscar Kokoschka, who became a loyal friend and created some remarkable portraits of the architect (Fig. 2).

Loos was very active—he loved nature and the world which, according to him, ought to remain just as it had appeared originally. He appreciated night life and surrounded himself with the prettiest girls in Vienna. He lived with, successively, four women: an actress, Lina Obertimpfler; a dancer, Bessie Bruce ("the epitome of an English girl"); another dancer, Elsie Altmann; and a photographer, Claire Beck. "That which is noble in a woman knows only one desire: that she hold on to her place by the side of the big, strong man. At present this desire can only be fulfilled if the woman wins the love of the man. This love makes her the man's subordinate."[13]

Loos traveled often and lived in many cities in Europe. In one sense he was more European than Viennese: he could be found in Paris, London, Prague or Berlin, at the Lido in Venice or on the Côte d'Azur, in Copenhagen, in Madrid, in Greece, in Italy and even in Algeria, for a conference, an exhibition, a caucus, a summer or winter holiday, to buy marble, to live, to see, to learn, and to understand his work. He was a man on the go, who came to understand the history of architecture by observing it *in situ*. In 1912, at the instigation of students of Otto Wagner who, at seventy years old, had just retired from teaching, Loos founded his own school. His students saw him as the successor to their old master. Despite certain disputed aspects, the program that he proposed remained strongly marked by classicism. For the teachings of specialized schools, which consisted "for one part: to adapt past styles to new needs; for another: to find a new style," Loos wanted to substitute the teaching of tradition. "At the beginning of the nineteenth century we abandoned tradition, it's at that point that I intend to renew it," because, he explained later, "the present is built on the past just as the past was built on the times that went before it."[14] His informal and anti-academic seminar took place in the heart of Vienna, near the buildings he cited as examples. The course was supposed to culminate every year in a long voyage, principally in Greece or Italy, which offered the possibility of experiencing the "superiority of classical antiquity."[15] This experience was interrupted by the war but was resumed in 1919 within the framework of Loos's office. Renowned architects such as Richard Neutra, Rudolf Schindler, and Paul Engelmann attended Loos's school and were strongly influenced by his ideas.

In the years that followed his return to Vienna, Adolf Loos acquired a reputation as a critic of functional objects and above all as an interior decorator. He started by working as an architect for Karl Mayreder, a professor of construction (Baukunst) at the Vienna Polytechnic, but he rapidly developed a private practice that kept him busy for about ten years, redesigning stores, cafes, and apartments.

His clientele was made up mostly of well-to-do intellectuals and luxury merchandisers who were fascinated by the artistic world. University professors, upper-level managers, important clothing designers, second-level patrons (as opposed to the grand patronage of bankers and industrialists who were already more open to the ideas of Secessionism) "had the merit, even if they were not always conscious of it, to finance an isolated adventurer" in his quest for an architecture of his time.[16] A large number of Loos's original clients remained loyal to him. The tailors Goldman & Salatsch, whose clothing store on Graben Street had been redesigned by Loos in 1898 (Figs. 26–27), eleven years later commissioned an apartment house, the ground floor of which was to be devoted to their shop. It is this building (Figs. 101–120) built from 1909 to 1911 on Michaelerplatz, across from the imperial palace of Vienna, that inscribed the name of the architect in the collective memory of the Viennese: it was called the Looshaus. The Looshaus's pared-down facades provoked discussions and disputes among his contemporaries, and the authorities even stopped construction for a while. In their eyes, such a building—because of its simplicity and consequent ugliness—disfigured the site.

At this point, Loos considered interior design a marginal activity. His ambitions were much greater, although he had very little built work. His first houses, the Villa Karma, near Geneva (1903–1906; Figs. 55–58) and the Steiner House in Vienna (1910; Figs. 59–61) rapidly became universal examples of rationalist architecture. His later work (see chapter 4), notably the Moller House in Vienna (1928; Figs. 74–78), is indicative of the rationalism that he had developed independent of the Modern Movement.

For Loos, the way that man builds houses explains the ethos of a people. Therefore, he approached each issue from an ethical rather than an aesthetic point of view, according a new importance to humane dignity, even down to the practical details of daily existence. His passion ran to the treatment of materials; he sought a formal language which would be the expression of function, spatially. To him, an architect was not at all a prince, a creator in the manner of Alberti, but "a mason who had learned Latin,"[17] like Palladio—a "mason" who espoused an aesthetic of truthful construction and utility. He admired Vitruvius, whose *Ten Books* (according to Kokoschka), were his bible. Kokoschka recounts that Loos took great pride in owning one of the first Italian editions of the work.[18]

Loos's urban houses were known for their traditional and bare aspect. Their plans and volumes evoked geometry long used by architects. Their discretion and strict regularity reflected the responsibility and desire Loos felt to surround people with peaceful clarity, rather than to subject them to the authority of an invasive genius.

After the end of the war and the declaration of the Austrian Republic (November 12, 1918), Loos began to actively intervene in the cultural politics of his country. In 1919, with Schönberg, Kraus and several others, he wrote "Guidelines for a Ministry of the Arts" which he edited himself. In 1920, he was named "Chief Architect of the Housing Department of the Commune of Vienna," an important position in the socialist administration of "Red Vienna." In the same year, he published his first book, *Ins leere gesprochen* (Spoken into the Void), a collection of the essays he had written between 1897 and 1900. In 1922, he participated in the international competition for the *Chicago Tribune* tower. The skyscraper he proposed, in the form of a Doric column, remains one of the principal reasons for the conflicting reception of his work (Figs. 140–141a). Also in 1922, he attended the congress on garden-cities in London. Having become a full member of the "Salon d'automne" which he visited regularly, in 1923 he showed the models for the Villa Moïssi (for the Lido in Venice, Figs. 92–93), the Grand Hotel Babylon (Nice; Fig. 146) and a group of twenty attached houses, which he called "villas" (for the Côte d'Azur; Fig. 121). Upon returning to Vienna, he participated with Peter Behrens, Joseph Frank, Josef Hoffmann and Oskar Strnad in a project to design workers' housing for seven hundred families. However, despite his sincere interest in modern workers' housing, for which he designed some remarkable projects, he resigned his job stating that he had too many ideological differences with the city bureaucracy.

Disappointed by his experience with the city of Vienna, he decided to move to Paris where he was already known. The French capitol remained the center of his activities until 1928. There he met the architects and artists Mallet-Stevens, Lurçat, Le Corbusier, Mondrian, Tzara....In 1925, he visited the famous *Exposition internationale des Arts Décoratifs et industrielles modernes* in which Le Corbusier (with his *Pavilion de L'Esprit nouveau*), Mallet-Stevens and Konstantin Melnikov participated. The same year, Loos organized a series of four conferences at the Sorbonne under the general title of "Man of Modern Nerves." Although he always found himself among the avant-garde of his day, he knew to differentiate himself and preserve his singularity.

Among the projects for Paris, his hotel on the Champs Elysées (Fig. 143) and office building containing a cinema on the Boulevard des Italiens (Fig. 150) evidenced his conception of urbanism. Blending in well with the existing fabric, Loos's buildings respected the form of the city.

His project for Josephine Baker (1927, Figs. 82–83), whom he had admired in the cabarets of Paris, is a masterpiece of enigmatic architecture. Oblong windows in the walls of its swimming pool allowed a glimpse of the swimmer's underwater ballet. This rediscovery of the feminine body and a voyeur's pleasure were indicative of Loos's eroticism, expressed in a poetic game of desire and confession.

Ultimately, Loos built only one house in Paris: that of Tristan Tzara in Montmartre (1926–1927; Figs. 69–73), an exercise in Loosian architecture and Dadaism. But the age of manifestoes was over for Tzara who, looking to live with his family, had chosen "this great architect, the only one today whose works are not photogenic, and whose expression is a school of depth and not a way to attain illusions of beauty."[19]

7   MODEL, MAUSOLEUM FOR ART HISTORIAN MAX DVORAK, 1921.
     Black granite from Sweden, interior fresco by Kokoschka.

In 1930, Loos celebrated his sixtieth birthday with a large number of European intellectuals. His renown had surpassed the constrained area of his architectural practice; several homages were given in publications in Paris, Prague and Vienna. W. Gropius, B. Taut, J. Itten, and J.-J.P. Oud joined A. Schönberg, A. Berg, A. Webern, E. Pound, S. Zweig, and J. Joyce to salute the "prophet" in person. "Using explosives in the guise of words and at the same time a productive nature in his works," wrote Zweig, "he showed in his creations so much somber, generous, and moderate harmony that he revealed a passionate and energetic rebellion of spirit, which alone has a chance of creating life. Mocked, hated, abused for forty years by all that is old and petrified, he ought, on the day of the sixtieth anniversary of his opinionated youth, to have the right to our thanks for his life and his ardor."[20]

In spite of everything, Loos was approaching the end of his life. Weakened by illness, almost deaf, he worked less and less. He died on August 23, 1933 at the Kalksbourg sanatorium near Vienna. In 1958 the city of Vienna erected a very simple tomb copied from a sketch that Loos himself had made in 1931 (Fig. 8). Thus was honored one who so well payed tribute to the architecture of eternal resting places.

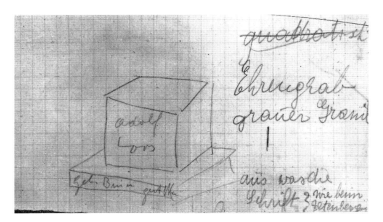

8   ADOLF LOOS: SKETCH OF HIS OWN TOMB (c. 1931).
     Loos's tomb in the Vienna cemetery was built from this sketch. The penciled-in notes specify that the tomb be a square of gray granite, engraved "like Altenberg's" (tomb of Peter Altenburg, designed by Loos in 1919).

9   ADOLF LOOS: SKETCH OF HIS OWN TOMB, WITH BUST BY FRANCIS WILLIS. NICE, 1931.
     Copy of original by Francis Willis.

Loos had always privileged man—in his house and in his grave—with the absolute values of our societies (as opposed to those linked to technological evolution) but his infamous definition should not be taken literally: "When we come across a mound in the wood, six feet long and three feet wide, raised to a pyramidal form by means of a spade, we become serious and something in us says: somebody lies buried here. *This is architecture*."[21] Loos made great use of allegory and symbolism. If he wrote that a tomb is architecture, it is the idea of a tomb that he is talking about—a high idea, sentient and inevitable, comparable to Nietzsche's aphorism that Loos inscribed in his second book, *Trotzdem*: "That which is decisive is produced in spite of everything." The tomb described by Loos is figurative, and not to be confused with the mausoleums in the cemeteries. His "mound...in the form of a pyramid" is situated in a forest. It is an abstract symbol, an irreducible architectural icon.

CHAPTER TWO
WRITINGS

Adolf Loos published two books. The first, *Spoken into the Void 1897–1900*, was a collection of essays written for the *Neue Freie Presse* for the Jubilee Exposition of 1898, as well as other critiques from the same period. Loos's intention to publish his writings was not realized until 1921 in Paris, through Crès and Company, Le Corbusier's publisher: "no German publishing house," he declared in his foreword, "dared to take it on in 1920. It was probably the only book in the last hundred years which was originally written in German, but which was published in France."[1] A second corrected edition appeared in 1932 from Brenner Editions in Innsbruck: the texts were presented in a different order and Loos had added "Potemkin City," an article published in 1898 in *Ver Sacrum*.[2] The second collection, *Trotzdem, 1900–1930*, appeared in 1931 (also from Brenner), followed by a second edition in the same year. *Trotzdem* contained, in particular, two essays of great influence: "Ornament and Crime," and "Architecture," which were republished by the author in 1908 and 1910.

Loos's trenchant, acerbic, and brilliant style assured him incontestable renown. He wrote with ease, in a style closer to speech than to writing. Joseph Rykwert, who wrote the preface for the Italian edition of Loos's writings (Milan, 1972), considered him (with the possible exception of Le Corbusier) the most important writer among architects of this century.

The essays collected in these two volumes do not constitute a systematic theory of architecture: ostensibly polemical, they reflect the fleeting nature of reality. These conditions explain certain liberties of expression and—when one reads the essays in order—the occasional dissonance or contradiction. Moreover, many of Loos's writings were published out of context, and were therefore misinterpreted or misunderstood, further complicating the reception of his ideas. Modern and postmodern architects alike may recognize a confirmation of their own ideas, but frequently they have missed the true meaning or the complex ironies in Loos's writing. Loos's criticisms of the 1898 Exposition, written just after his return from the United States, bear little resemblance and often contradict what he wrote thirty years later, at a more experienced and mature point in his career. The formulation of a coherent and consistent image from such a complex body of work could only be attributed to a reader's bias.

Is Ornament a Crime?

Most Loosian scholars consider "Ornament and Crime" to be his identity card. Others see this text as a terrible anathema, a radical and puritan manifesto, and the beginning, in some way, of the suppression of ornamentation in modern architecture. Among Loos's writings, *Ornament and Crime* is, without doubt, the most famous. On January 21, 1910, the author "lectured on this subject 'for nearly a half-hour' to the *Akademischer Verband fur Literatur und Musik*[3] of Vienna [the *Fremden Blatt* of January 22 reports on the lecture]."[4] He repeated the lecture in 1913 in Vienna and in Copenhagen. These lectures were followed by a French translation of an essay under the same title in *Les Cahiers d'aujourd'hui* of June 1913, and were also released in the second volume of *L'Esprit nouveau* (November 15, 1920). The text did not appear in German until 1929 (*Frankfurter Zeitung*, October 24), after which it was republished many times. This brief historical account rectifies the widespread theory that the suppression of ornament in modern architecture was in part a consequence of an article published in Vienna in 1908, under the title of "Ornament and Crime." One would search in vain for this article which, in reality, does not exist. It should be dated from 1920, the year of its publication in *L'Esprit nouveau*.

Regardless, what had Loos said? He had stated the essential parts of his criticism of the architects and artists of the Secession: "I have discovered the following truth and present it to the world: *cultural evolution is equivalent to the removal of ornament from articles in daily use*."[5] This phrase, the only one in italics in pages of text, which limits the suppression of ornament to functional objects (with several reservations), underlines, above all, the anti-secessionist intention of the "pamphlet." Loos's criticism makes sense only in this precise context, which may have been the reason why he lectured only once on this subject. He did not, however, insist on the suppression of all architectural ornament: it is clear that he does not compare "the superfluous" ornamentation of the Secession (and generally of Art Nouveau) with the "grammar" of classical ornament—of which, on the contrary, he approved and which he practiced, as will be seen in chapter four—nor with the geometric decoration inherent in the use of semi-precious materials, of which he made great use, particularly on the interior.

However, outside Vienna and divorced from the causes that engendered it, the initial meaning of this essay, with its provocative title, was altered. In Paris, it was received as a purist manifesto that demanded the total suppression of ornament ("Ornament IS crime"). This slippage of meaning: the identification of ornament in general with crime—this "crime" which, in Loos's pamphlet, appeared a sort of "ornament" of discussion—even shocked the author himself. In 1924, he wrote in "Ornament and Education": "I affirmed twenty-six years ago that the evolution of humanity would cause ornament to disappear from functional objects, an evolution which would follow its ineluctable and logical path....But I never thought like the purists who pushed this reasoning to the absurd, that ornament should be systematically abolished. It is only where the passage of time makes it disappear that it cannot be reborn."[6] It is clear that if such a text had been read as a manifesto in favor of a stripped architecture, the text had been read incorrectly, or out of context.

Considering the distance that separates us from Loos's time, interest in an analysis of the architect today relies on his conception of ornament as the sign of an uncultured state. It is what underlines his startling comparison between the tattooing of Papuans, the beginning of art, and the tattooing of modern man, the mark of criminal degeneracy.[7] Loos accused his contemporaries of using ornament on their furniture, their buildings, and their clothes as a way of masking the mediocrity of their culture and their social condition. He reproached them not only for misrepresenting their principles, but for plastering their bodies, attaching borrowed facades to their buildings, for transforming—in the eyes of society—their "desert" into a "prosperous country." But if he criticized ornament—that which is added to a composition to give it value, a fleeting glitter—he approved, on the contrary, of decoration considered as a set of rules (issuing from properly worked materials and from the "grammar" of classical language) that he agreed to observe so as to render architecture more palatable. He also saw this classical grammar as capable of conveying, simply and directly, the identity—ministry, monument, bourgeois villa, worker's housing, etc.—of a structure.

Loos's position on clothing clarifies his position on ornament. He conceived of clothing as a neutral envelope that has neither to be the sign of an artificial personality nor a manner of dissimulation. The outfit should be of a revelatory "transparence"; it should, by its discretion and simplicity, reflect a truthfulness and purity in man. English dress represented, in Loos's eyes, the clothing that was best adapted to the modern metropolitan man. Having arrived at this urban asceticism, modern man has, from then on, no need for ornamentation. By dressing correctly and still preserving his integrity, he can use the elements of *decoration*, whose mission is no longer to dissimulate or mask, but function as the signs of complicity and adhesion with the common cultural bases of society. Loos's modern man is a master of "meta-language": the comprehensive language born of the utilization of these signs.

In reality, the opposition between ornament and decoration uncovers another, much more profound, which distinguishes the ephemeral from the durable. Loos likened the incessant renewing of ornaments (under the pretext of innovation) to the effect of a spectacle, to fashion, and to seduction reducing the durability of objects. "The functional object endures as long as the material from which it is made; its modern value comes from its solidity. When a functional object suffers an ornamental digression, its durability is abridged, because then it is submitted to fashion....Functional objects such as fabrics or carpets, whose endurance is limited, remain submissive to fashion and, consequently, are ornamented."[8]

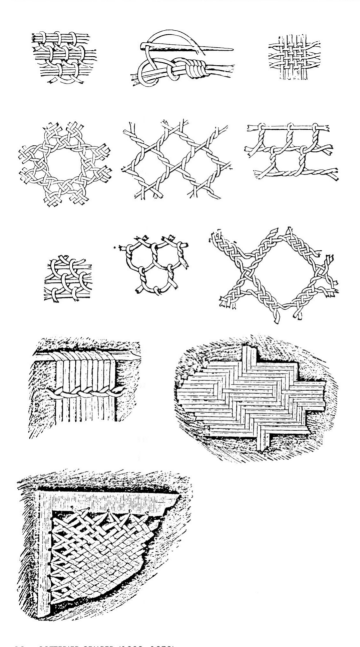

10   GOTTFRIED SEMPER (1803–1879).
     Weaving techniques (*Der Stil*, Munich, 1863: pp. 174–177).

11   GOTTFRIED SEMPER, CARL VON HASENAUER (1833–1894): HOFSCHAUSPIELHAUS, VIENNA.
Three bays of side elevation, 1873. For Semper, weaving and building were linked by an
analogy between clothing a body and cladding a building, a relationship on which he based
much of his work. In 1898, Loos wrote an article addressing the issue of cladding, continuing
in the Semperian tradition.

Elaborating on this argument (the more immutable an object, the less ornament it has),
Loos gave women the right to ornament, for erotic significance: "Woman covered herself,
she became a riddle to man, in order to implant in his heart the desire for the riddle's solution....It is an unnatural love. If it were natural, the woman would be able to approach the
man naked. But the naked woman is unattractive to the man. She may be able to arouse a
man's love, but not to keep it."[9] Generally, Loos linked eroticism to a need for adornment
and ornamentation which were considered elementary, artistic expressions. But this need
should be repressed when it becomes a question of producing conscious, and consequently,
superior art. Art, having passed the stage of creative intuition, must elevate itself above
repression of primitive impulses; its reduction to ornament was denounced as a sign of the
immorality of the age. In the same sense, architecture cannot be ornamented without losing
its strength.

Finally, in the name of a rationalist, cultural tradition Loos criticized ornament. He was
opposed to the fleeting nature of successive "revivals" in the second half of the nineteenth
century, and imputed them with the same ephemeral and superfluous character of the orna-

mental works of the Secession. On the other hand, he admired the atemporality of the classical language. For him, the persistence of the same formal typology from the Renaissance to the neoclassicism of the beginning of the nineteenth century was not a *revival* but a *tradition*, and relied on forms that had resisted the fluctuations of fashion and that reflected, consequently, a deep and durable modernity. Forcing the terms a little, one could say that, for Loos, western classicism revealed less a *culture* than a *nature*: it is in the natural environment where western man moves and recognizes himself. Classical architecture did not bring about *ornament*; its traits were simple and universal enough to encompass Ancient Greek and Roman as well as the Renaissance, Palladio and Schinkel. This rational classicism nourished in Loos, as we will see, a great sensitivity to the essentials that went far beyond signifiers. Certain historians have given a name to this tendency: they call it "modern classicism."[10]

Towards an Architecture without the Avant-Garde

"Architecture," which appeared in the collection *Trotzdem*, is justly considered one of Loos's most influential and widely-known essays. It contains the essence of his criticism on the architecture of his age, as well as his thoughts on the art of modern construction. Less celebrated and radical than "Ornament and Crime," "Architecture" was first presented in October 1910, at the Chamber of Architects in Berlin, and was the subject of a second lecture during the same year at the Art Society of Hanover. A short excerpt appeared in *Der Sturm* on December 15, 1910, but the first publication of the whole text was in French in *Les Cahiers d'aujourd'hui* of December 1912, under the title "Architecture and Modern Style."

To define modern architecture, Loos divided the past into two unequal and opposing periods: from classical antiquity to the first half of the nineteenth century; and from the second half of the nineteenth to contemporary times. The second period, which he criticized harshly, was presented as the antithesis of the first, and, simultaneously, as the antithesis of his personal conception of architecture. In this way did Loos historically justify his preference for classical antiquity, which had been abandoned and subjected to diverse eclecticisms and revivals during the second half on the nineteenth century.

He began with the problem of culture, which he defined as "that balance of man's inner and outer being which alone guarantees rational thought and action."[11] For Loos, the history of humanity had never known an age without culture, and culture had been developing consistently and continually along the way. But in the second half of the nineteenth century, architects—as well as most city dwellers—had decided to live without culture; that is, outside of the spirit of their age, looking to the past and the future, ahead and behind, but not to the present.

opposite page:

12   JOHANN BERNHARD FISCHER VON ERLACH (1656–1723): CHURCH OF SAINT CHARLES BORROMEO.
      Entwurfe einer historischer Architektur, Vienna, 1721: book IV, plate XII.
      Similarly insistent symmetry can be found in many of Loos's buildings (see Figs. 134–137, 138, 149).

13   KARL FRIEDRICH SCHINKEL (1781–1841): COMMEMORATIVE MONUMENT FOR FREDERICK II, BERLIN, 1829.
      Sammlung Architektonischer Entwürfe, folio no. 115, Berlin, 1833.
      The column of Trajan—a monument of no practical purpose whatsoever—was often used by Fischer von Erlach and Schinkel in the 18th and 19th centuries. Loos paid tribute to its symbolic value and monumental character in his competition entry for the *Chicago Tribune* (Figs. 140–141).

His criticism of the period was very violent: "Nervous vanity was alien to the old masters," whose standardized house types pleased everyone. Houses of Loos's time, on the contrary, pleased only two people: the owner and the architect. The "false prophets," he explained, gathered the debris of all the cultures, and crammed them into museums and took it upon themselves to catalog the ornamentation, and the study of styles became a serious diversion. Unlike "the old masters [for whom] the drawing was merely a means of communicating with the craftsmen who were carrying out the work," architects of Loos's day gained all their knowledge from books and demanded that the workers reproduce in one day styles from twenty different centuries and twenty different peoples. "The art of building has been degraded by the architect into a graphic art."

After having exhausted the ancient ornaments, the architects set about inventing new ones, which represented, in Loos's eyes, the height of a lack of culture: "Now they believe that they have found the style of the twentieth century. But that is not the style of the twentieth century. There are many things which show the style of the twentieth century in its pure form. They are those products whose producers have not been placed under the supervision of those who wish to distort our culture." Thus he formulated his stance towards decorative arts and the architecture of his time, a stance evident in his classification of the past into two opposing periods.

Loos attempted to classify the respective areas of art and architecture. He defined art as the personal affair of the artist—oriented to the future, distracting man from his daily comforts: art is by its essence revolutionary. Conversely, a house cannot be a matter of personal taste; unlike a work of art it responds to a practical need. The architect must answer to the whole world. Seen simply as a form of shelter and accommodation, a house must respond to a set of fairly conservative yet universal values.[12] Nevertheless, Loos recognized that some of an architect's repertoire could approach art: the monument (*Denkmal*) and the tomb. "Everything else that fulfils a function is to be excluded from the domain of art." Loos felt that architecture ought not to look for innovation, but should satisfy the exigencies of humanity, such as they are posed, in the most basic way possible.

Loos next introduced an idea about the way that architecture should communicate: "Architecture arouses sentiments in man. The architect's task therefore, is to make those sentiments more precise. The room has to be comfortable; the house has to look habitable. The law courts must appear as a threatening gesture towards secret vice. The bank must declare: here your money is secure and well looked after by honest people. The architect can only achieve this if he establishes a relationship with those buildings which have hitherto created this sentiment in man."[13]

Loos saw permanent contact with the spirit of the world (*Weltgeist*) as the primordial condition of modernity. The architect must be aware of the age, the place, the needs and the climate, but he must also respect the traditions which fix the forms. Only the appearance of new practical needs, new problems, and new techniques or rules would justify a change in forms. When Loos spoke of the renewal or modification of rules he made no allusion to an anti-historicist rupture such as the one instigated by the Modern Movement, but to the evolution of a tradition anchored in the architecture of antiquity. He called himself a traditionalist, but he was most closely linked to a deep classicism that did not restrict itself to the limitation of past forms. "But every time the minor architects who use ornament move architecture away from its grand model, a great architect is at hand to guide them back to antiquity. Fischer von Erlach in the south, Schlüter in the north, were justifiably the great masters of the eighteenth century. And at the threshold to the nineteenth century stood Schinkel. We have forgotten him. May the light of this towering figure shine on our forthcoming generation of architects!"

The radically different meaning that Loos on the one hand, and avant-garde architects of the nineteen-twenties on the other, accorded the word *modern*, here takes on a new significance. For Loos, to be modern was to belong to one's time and, *consequently*, to tradition, an alive and real past. In addition, this modern was not universal: what was modern for one was not necessarily modern for everyone. The architect was neither the connoisseur nor the challenger of modernity. The Viennese did not have the same conception of modern, "did not live in the same era" as the peasant from an Austrian mountain village. In his writings, as in his built work, Loos reconciled social and technological changes with a respect for tradition. Ironically, in an age which challenged the past, Loos continued to include history in his conception of modern.

CHAPTER THREE
RENOVATIONS: APARTMENTS, STORES, CAFES

Loos's apartment and store renovations constitute the majority of his realized work. Even when committed to larger projects, he never gave up "decorating," his principle activity at the beginning of his career. But Loos never considered it an architectural activity: "I will continue to furnish [in the sense of all aspects of interior design]...stores, cafes and apartments," he wrote in 1903. "But decorating lodgings has nothing to do with architecture. I subsisted on it because it is something I *know how to do*. The same was true in America, at one point, when I provided for my needs by washing dishes."[1] (The tone of this remark attests to Loos's critical manner and curt, abrasive style.) If, with these interior renovations, Loos considered himself basically a "guide for strangers, strangers to culture,"[2] he was still quite passionate about all the material aspects of daily life: furniture, functional objects, clothing....Whatever one thinks of his houses, one can never take them for simple envelopes of masonry, strangers to their contents. They reveal, on the contrary, Loos's expertise in the art of arrangement—the integration of circulation, built-in furniture, and cladding—which he considered to be the primordial role of "living" conditions.

"To furnish lodgings" was understood to be synonymous with "giving advice." Loos thought it inappropriate to create an apartment the way one creates a work of art, imposing the design as a finished piece on the client. In *The Poor Little Rich Man*,[3] written in 1900, Loos recounts the misadventures of an owner who made an architect famous for asking him to transform his home into a work of art, no matter what the cost of renovation. Great was the owner's deception: he discovers that he can neither change nor add to the architect's creation. This fable explains Loos's criticism of Art Nouveau, and it also permits us to measure the extent (or rather, the limit) of his intervention in the private life of his clients. As he wrote, not without pride, each client "lives in his *own* lodgings, according to his own personality. Mitigated, it is true, by my advice."[4]

American interiors and English atmosphere influenced Loos heavily, particularly at the beginning of his career. Richard Neutra, who studied with Loos before the first world war, wrote that Loos had brought certain features of the work of H. H. Richardson to Vienna:[5] obviously false oak beams and fireplaces of exposed brick masonry. According to Neutra, it was the first time that European forms were inspired by an American style.[6] Loos often employed these characteristic features during the first ten years of his work, but more important was his appreciation for the subtlety of Richardson's stripped interiors and their classic simplicity, when compared to other apartments of the same era.

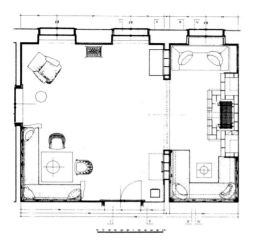

14   LOOS APARTMENT: VIENNA, 1903.
      Plan, sitting room. Drawing: 1946.

In certain cases, Loos made structural modifications to existing housing, to achieve continuity between the living room and the dining room. Looking to combine a reception hall
and more intimate spaces, he did not hesitate to introduce false ceilings to reduce and
define the volumes. His willingness to make the most out of a space was subordinate to
the conviction that different rooms required different heights according to their function.
Loos, nourished by English and American models—C.F.A. Voysey, M.H. Baillie Scott or
McKim, Mead & White—greatly developed this principle when he himself started to
design houses.

Loos's apartment renovations have a certain number of characteristics in common: a
predominance of unified surfaces (walls and draperies), an axial arrangement of space, and
an elimination of ornament, compensated for by the presence of certain abstract patterns
inherent in the cladding materials. Wood, veined marble, mirrors, leather, fabric, and carpets were combined to create an atmosphere of warmth—whose "aura" could not be cap-
tured by photography. Refusing all formal innovation in functional objects, Loos chose
simple and traditional furniture that he rarely had designed himself, adding a conservative
aspect to his interiors: "To design a new dining room chair is for me a folly, a completely
superfluous folly, linked to a loss of time and energy. The dining room chair from
Chippendale's time was perfect. It was *the* solution. It cannot be surpassed. Like our fork,
like our foil, like our screw-driver."[7] He sought to create comfortable and beautiful apartments, without the least intention of seducing the readers of the illustrated, avant-garde

15   LOOS APARTMENT.
Fireplace niche, seen from sitting room. Photo: 1909.

16   LOOS APARTMENT.
Fireplace niche. Photo: c. 1909.

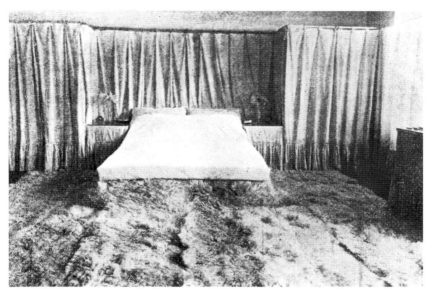

17 LOOS APARTMENT.
Bedroom of Loos's wife, Lina. Photo: 1903.

journals. It was enough for him to respond to the wishes of his clientele: well-off intellectuals and rich merchants, whose social status and cultural aspirations were close to his own. Regardless, these interiors are counted among Loos's most important contributions to twentieth-century architecture.

After his first marriage in 1902, Loos settled into an apartment on the fifth floor of an old Viennese building (Bösendorfestrasse 3) which he occupied until his death. The living room (also used as the dining room) and the adjacent room with the fireplace were reconstructed in 1958 at the Historical Museum of Vienna. With his wife's bedroom, featured in 1903 in *Kunst*, a journal edited by Peter Altenberg, these rooms—Loos's own lodgings—represent the purified expression of the renovations he did for his clientele.

The two spaces of the living area were differentiated by ceiling height, and the boundary between the two was marked by a large opening on axis with the fireplace (Figs. 14, 15, 16). As the public sphere of private life, the materials, furniture and general scale of these spaces expressed the occupants' social image. The two spaces were distinguished from each other both psychologically and functionally: the smaller was more intimate, with an exposed-brick fireplace and two adjacent alcoves for fireside reading and relaxation. The ceiling, lowered to the height of the opening, was crossed by a series of false beams which visually link the two rooms; the ceiling of the larger space was marked by these beams as well, and coffered wood paneling covered the walls. Daily life here attained a laconic, classical spirit.

The white room that Loos designed for Lina, his blonde, blue-eyed, nineteen-year-old wife, was the most intimate place in the house (Fig. 17). The white walls, the white draperies and the white angora sheepskins created a sensual and delicate fluidity; every object in the room was white. Even the closets were concealed behind pale linen drapes. This was an architecture of silence, of a sentimental and erotic approach. Its contrast with the more public living spaces attests to a method of composition that was strictly governed by the psychological status of each room.

Loos's renovations tended to include mostly reception rooms and bedrooms. In certain projects, he entirely redesigned the existing space, making major structural modifications (Duschnitz and Mandl houses; Villas Strasser and Reitler). Unfortunately, little is known of Loos's structural interventions; there are few photos and no drawings; the design was born directly from experience. The diversity of Loos's work and of his clients, the changes *a posteriori*, and the lack of plans, make all analysis incomplete.

Among Loos's renovations of dining rooms, that of Paul Khuner's apartment (Vienna, 1907; Fig. 18) embodied a simplicity of form, a sobriety in the working of the materials, and traditional furnishings. The ceiling's checkerboard of false beams, the walls' square grid of wood panels, and the pattern of the carpet all worked to create an illusion of depth, stopping just before the tapestry and curtains that cover the wall and windows.

The same effect was created in Emil Löwenbach's sumptuous dining room (Vienna, 1913–1914; Fig. 20), with a coffered ceiling, a floor of deep-colored wood, and wall paneling of clear marble. A geometric pattern of lights in the ceiling coffers neutralized its somber and "heavy" aspect, and guided the eye to the large mirror on the far wall, which reflected the room.

opposite page:

18   P. KHUNER APARTMENT: VIENNA, 1907.
      Dining room. Photo: 1930.

19   VILLA STRASSER: VIENNA, 1918–1919.
      Dining room. Photo: 1930. A frieze runs just below the ceiling, on walls of book-matched marble.

20   E. LÖWENBACH APARTMENT: VIENNA, 1913.
     Dining room. Photo: 1930.

The atmosphere of the dining room in the Villa Strasser (Vienna, 1918–1919; Fig. 19), however, was very different. The simplicity of the smooth, white, plaster ceiling contrasted with the floor, decorated with loops and rhombuses. The walls were clad with greenish porous onyx, whose book-matched panels created geometric figures. A frieze of antique figures circled the room, just below the ceiling—a decorative touch justified (for Loos) by its geometric rigor and classical origin. The room was furnished traditionally, with pieces in cherry wood. This room, renovated at the end of World War I, did not even hint at the radicalism of the *tabula rasa* recommended by the purists of the 1920s.

The living room of Dr. Joseph Vogl (Pilsen, 1929; Fig. 21) is typical of the manner in which Loos renovated reception areas. The room was dominated by an exposed brick fireplace flanked by veined marble pillars and topped by a large mirror divided into several squares. The symmetry of this ensemble contrasts with the less ordered positioning of the furniture.

The continuous space of Leo Brummel's living room (Pilsen, 1929; Fig. 22), offers an example of a renovation in an era when luxurious materials were limited. Somewhat in the manner of the de Stijl neoplasticists, Loos used the contrast of lively and brilliant colors like green, red, black and white, with more somber shades of bronze and silver, to animate

21   VOGL APARTMENT: PILSEN, 1929.
Sitting room. Photo: 1930. Compare the light fixtures, fireplace, mirror, and chairs with those in the
Knize clothing store, Paris (Fig. 32).

22   LEO BRUMMEL APARTMENT: PILSEN, 1929.
Photo from 1930. Note the lacquered wood mouldings and the Egyptian footstools, which, from 1899
Loos used in his interiors.

23   HANS BRUMMEL APARTMENT.
Bedroom. Photo: 1930.

this interior. Like Kulka, he was convinced that "all natural colors go together, as we can certify in the art of primitive races, in national costumes, carpets, etc., but also in flags and coats of arms. The elaboration of theories about the combination of colors can only concern the chemical industry."[8] Loos, therefore, differed from Kandinsky and the teachings of the Bauhaus on the psychology and the physiology of colors.

In general, Loos demonstrated total liberty in the renovations of private interiors, obeying no previous style. In comparing two similar elements—twelve years apart—the marble column in the Villa Strasser (1918–1919; Fig. 24) and the encased column in the Moller House (1927–1928; Fig. 25), it is clear that Loos passed from classical to modern, but neither "evolved" nor contradicted himself. He obeyed a liberal concept of the home: as a conservative entity, it should respond to one criterion only—the well-being of its inhabitants. The architect should remain in the background, impose nothing, and subordinate his desires to those of the client: "the modern spirit demands individuality. That means, in general, that the king furnishes his home like a king, the bourgeois like a bourgeois, and the peasant like a peasant; and in particular, that every king, every bourgeois, and every peasant expresses his own characteristic qualities in the furnishings of his home."[9]

Loos's designs for luxury shops proved his ability to create understated opulence, even in the smallest of spaces, as well as his mastery of weaving his work into the commercial urban code. He renovated fifteen shops, ten of which were clothing stores. Throughout his

24   VILLA STRASSER: VIENNA, 1918–1919.
      Sitting room. Photo: 1930.

25   MOLLER HOUSE: VIENNA, 1927–1928.
      Stair, seen from sitting room. Photo: 1930.

26   GOLDMAN & SALATSCH MEN'S CLOTHING STORE: VIENNA, 1898–1903.
Ground floor c. 1901.

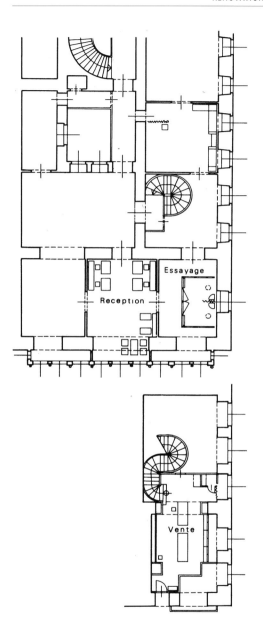

27   GOLDMAN & SALATSCH MEN'S CLOTHING STORE.
     Plan drawings of renovation by B. Rukschcio and R. Schachel.

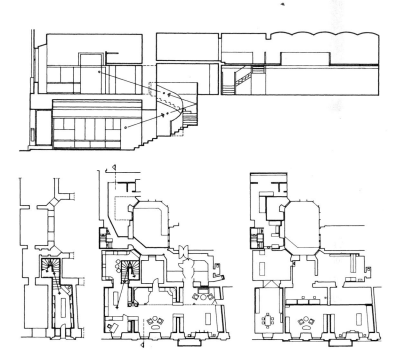

opposite page:

28   SIGMUND STEINER PLUME AND FEATHER STORE: VIENNA, 1906–1907.
       Fake beams on ceiling. Photo: 1930.

29   KNIZE CLOTHING STORE: VIENNA, 1910–1913.
       Section and plan drawings of renovation by D. Worbs.

this page:

30   KNIZE CLOTHING STORE.
       Facade in black marble. Photo: 1986.

31   KNIZE CLOTHING STORE.
First floor. Photo: 1930. Polyhedral brass light, frequently used by Loos.

life, Loos showed a particular interest in the world of clothes and fashion. He was always remarkably dressed in expensive but tasteful outfits furnished by his clients Goldman & Salatsch. Moreover, his thoughts on the relationship between fashion and society also appeared in his concept of architecture: just as "he who is dressed in a modern manner is one who is least conspicuous," likewise "the house had to look inconspicuous."[10]

The stores that Loos designed (in existing buildings) were all situated in the center of the city. The generally limited space on the ground floor called for the creation of a second floor. Because the disposition of spaces was irregular and even unsuitable to the well-running of an establishment, mastery of the sites became a necessity, requiring inventive use of space, and deft and clever use of optics to "enlarge" the interiors.

By surmounting these odds Loos arrived finally at a general principle of formal regularity. By allying a practical spirit and English elegance with rare textures and finely worked materials, and by challenging all contemporary models, he fascinated and astounded his clients as well as his critics. The intransigent order that reigned in his stores was especially notable in an era of stylistic and ornamental flourishes.

The facades of these shops were advertisements—from the street, the shops had (like Loos's guidelines for modern fashion) to stand out, to draw attention, to "sell" themselves.

32   ADOLF LOOS WITH FRITZ WOLFF (?) IN KNIZE STORE, PARIS, 1927–1928.
On mantle, a cubist bust of Loos by Zamoyski.

33   SIGMUND STEINER PLUME AND FEATHER STORE: VIENNA, 1906–1907.
      Facade in polished Skyros marble, convex shop windows. Photo: c. 1920.

Loos used exquisite materials—marble from Skyros and black granite from Sweden—mixed with large glass surfaces framed in rare woods or leather. These spectacular facades fronted interiors of precious woods, ingenious display cases, custom-designed fixtures, metallic finishes and large sections of mirror, all combining in a dazzling yet refined kaleidoscopic effect. Loos's success was proved by the loyalty of his clients. Knize & Company entrusted him with the renovations of all three of their stores: Vienna (1910), Berlin (1924) and Paris (1927).

Historians have always considered the Goldman & Salatsch men's clothing store (Vienna, 1898–1903; Figs. 26–27) as the utmost expression of Loos's refined sensibilities: "Nothing in this store can be called, strictly speaking, ornamental," wrote Pevsner in 1936, "the value of this work depends entirely on the materials and the dignity of the proportions. The decorative effect of the frieze is attained by the introduction of convex curves and a rapid rhythm of vertical and horizontal intersections."[11] The ground floor was extremely narrow, but a beautiful stair led clients to the more spacious upper floor. Loos used strychnine wood (*Schlangenholz*), a durable material, paired with shiny copper fittings. All the surfaces were smooth and polished, and were multiplied by mirrors.

Loos achieved the same effect in Sigmund Steiner's feather boutique (Vienna, 1906–1907) employing an entirely orthogonal design, completely devoid of ornament. The cladding of the walls, cabinetry, and windows in satinwood was elegant and austere. A mirror on the back wall doubled the small space of the ground floor. Globe-shaped lights hung on copper chains from exposed wood beams. A lack of structural justification for these beams (Fig. 28), nailed to the white, roughly-cast ceiling, inevitably raised questions about the integrity of the design and its contradictions with Loos's writings, which spoke harshly against useless ornament and false materials. Yet he used false beams, non-load-bearing marble columns, and space-enhancing mirrors. From the point of view of the modernists who insisted upon truth and transparency in structure, Loos's creations were aberrations. Loos defended himself by pointing out that although they played no structural role, his beams were real wood and his columns were real marble. Additionally, these elements were not ornamental, they did not aim to lie, and they were not useless: they were part of the architecture. Loos's objective was not absolute rationality; he designed spaces appropriate for the clothing, feather, or jewelry trade, with the secular language of those he called "his ancestors."

At Knize (Vienna, 1910–1913; Figs. 29–31), a mirror at the turn in the staircase offered a glimpse of the upper floor, and attracted customers to the main premises of the store. The shop's narrow facade was clad in smooth, polished granite from Sweden, and reddish cherry wood and deep-colored oak dominated the interior. The subtle classicism, geometric decoration, select choice of materials, and fine craftsmanship spoke of the social status of Loos's clients, tailors to the Court of Vienna.

34   MANZ BOOKSHOP: VIENNA, 1912.
     Facade in black marble and mahogany, letters in granite. Photo: 1986.

35   HUGO & ALFRED SPITZ JEWELLERS: VIENNA, 1918.
     Elevation recreated by B. Rukschcio and R. Schachel.

In Paris, at Champs Elysées no. 146, the store window of Knize's subsidiary featured a sculpture of a polo player to attract a certain class of clientele. The shop's front door and counters were mahogany, and the walls and the columns of the main salon were clad in clear cipolin marble, to contrast with the plush black carpet. Lighting was both natural— from a large bay window overlooking the avenue—and artificial, from copper dodecahedrons, like those used in the Vienna store (Fig. 31). Lacquered bamboo chairs and tables added a note of gaiety to this fashionable store for amateur sportsmen.[12]

Because of the architecture and the materials used, the facade of Sigmund Steiner's feather boutique (Vienna, 1906–1907; Fig. 33) was Loos's most subtle. The symmetrical facade made quite a sensation, according to an article by an important critic of the period, Ludwig Hevesi.[13] The facade was clad in a rosy polished marble from Skyros whose slabs Loos had chosen himself. The frames of the large convex windows, and the name of the boutique (affixed to the marble) were copper. Unfortunately, the name was virtually illegible, but Loos insisted that it was more important to use materials and symbols to project an image than to create a legible sign.[14]

It was in the same spirit, a few years later, that he designed the facade of Hugo & Alfred Spitz's jewelry store (Vienna, 1918; Fig. 35); a tripartite composition with ionic columns of veined white marble framed the front door and the windows of deep-colored wood. The capitals and bases of the two columns (non load-bearing) and the copings of the pilasters were bronze. Although the facade was basically a layer applied to the existing wall of the building, it had a severe but impressive character and showcased the firm's wares to advantage. As always, Loos chose his palate of materials to best convey the character of each client.

Among all of Loos's renovations, the Cafe Museum (Vienna, 1899; Figs. 36–37) was the most immediately discussed. It occupied the ground floor of a building situated between the Beaux Arts Academy, the Opera, the Artists' House and Olbrich's Secession Exhibition Building, which had just been finished (Figs. 3–4). Because of the location, the cafe's clientele were painters, architects, and musicians, and the project was designed with them in mind. However, Loos forbade all decorative elements with artistic connotations: he strove to create a place dominated by the rational aesthetic of useful things. Because of its radical, stripped-down look, the new establishment was dubbed "Nihilist Cafe," much to Loos's satisfaction. He was not aiming at originality, but at reproducing the Viennese cafe of 1830, a time still sensitive to the classical tradition. What was built expressed a modernity very different from the neighboring Secession building. The Cafe Museum's large smooth surfaces were recovered in rough cast stone and stripped of ornament, as much on the inside as on the outside. This cold whiteness produced a somewhat shocking but timeless purity. Even the band of copper in the vaulted ceiling in the grand L-shaped salon was functional—it hid the electrical conduits.

36 CAFE MUSEUM, VIENNA: 1899.
    Referred to as the "Nihilist Cafe" because of its severity.

37 CAFE MUSEUM.
    Interior seen from entrance. Photo: 1899.

38   CAFE MUSEUM.
      Chair built per Loos's specifications.

Loos was especially interested in the woods he designed with and specified. The pivotal point—literally and figuratively—of the Cafe Museum, was its mahogany bar, surrounded by mirrors. Loos chose to use a Thonet chair with an astonishingly slim back and an unusual ellipsoidal seat for better weight distribution (Fig. 38), because it wed classical tradition with practicality: "Since the decline of the Western Roman Empire," wrote Loos in October 1898, "there has been no era that has thought and felt more classically than ours....Look at the Thonet chair! Without decoration, embodying the sitting habits of a whole era, is it not born out of the same spirit as the Greek chair with its curved feet and its backrest?"[15] Even the cafe's round tables, whose four curved legs of wood held a slab of marble, were reminiscent of the form of the Greek three-legged stool. From the beginning of his career, Loos espoused the negation of formal innovation and the rediscovery of the stripped classicism of 1800. "The level of culture that mankind maintained in classical antiquity can no longer simply be eradicated from man's mind," he wrote during the work on the Cafe Museum. "Classical antiquity was and is the mother of all subsequent periods of culture."[16]

The "American Bar" in Kärntner Durchgang (Vienna, 1908; Fig. 39) is generally considered a masterpiece of interior design and an exemplary adaptation of an American "institution" to a Viennese milieu. Oskar Kokoschka enthusiastically described its inimitable atmosphere: "As soon as one passed under its sign, hanging at an angle, and decorated

39 "AMERICAN BAR": VIENNA, 1908.
Interior. A landscape quickly replaced Gustav Jagerspacher's portrait of Altenburg, the poet. Loos had commissioned Jagerspacher to paint his friend. Photo: c. 1909.

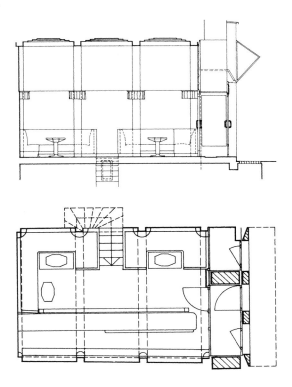

40   "AMERICAN BAR."
Section and plan drawings by B. Rukschcio and R. Schachel.

with pieces of blue, white and deep-red glass like in a western, the filtered light from the ceiling's marble coffers and the undersides of the translucent tables gave you the sense of well-being. You sipped your drink like a disillusioned pleasure-seeker. The ice cubes in your glass seemed to warm themselves in the magnificent evening light which filtered through the onyx squares of the fan-light over the narrow door. The tranquil discretion of this bar permitted one to lose the agitation which already pervaded the other cafes."[17]

The most amazing aspect of the Kärntnerbar was that Loos had fit a long counter, two booths, and three octagonal tables into such a tiny space (6.15 by 4.45 meters, or 20.5 by 15 feet) (Fig. 40), and still managed to create an intimate yet spacious atmosphere. His palate of different classical materials helped: veined, honey-yellow marble for the ceiling coffers, deep mahogany for the bar, the tables, and the wall cladding, black leather for the booths, and shiny copper, onyx, and large mirrors along the tops of the walls, which infinitely multiplied the ceiling coffers. Regular forms and noble materials: Loos dedicated this particularly successful work to his friend Peter Altenberg, a poet of pure and laconic style, whose portrait by Gustav Jagerspacher hung on the back wall of the Kärntnerbar.

Most of Loos's interiors are characterized by the use of abstract decorative elements, either by choice, by patterns inherent in materials (veining in marble, grains in wood), or else drawn from classical vocabulary. Flat bands of geometric motifs crowned the wood cabinetry and cladding of his stores. In one of his cafes and in various private reception rooms, Loos applied cast Renaissance or classical friezes to the wall, just below the ceiling line (Fig. 19). Did this contradict his own ideas about the necessity of removing ornament from functional objects? First, we must consider that furniture integrated with structure and wall paneling cannot be truly considered furniture. Conversely, if Loos was opposed to the use of fake ornament from the past as well as to the invention of superfluous ornament, he still deeply respected the grammar of classical ornament—considered an integral part of the classical language of architecture—and made a significant distinction between *decoration* and *ornamentation*. For Loos *decoration*—the purposeful use of simple forms and the honest use of materials—was indispensable in his otherwise spare constructions. The "decoration" that he introduced to an apartment or a store belonged to our century, in defiance of the ornate historicity of the second half of the nineteenth century, and was ahead of its time. It was not until the twenties and thirties that architects would employ pure forms and would unquestioningly clad walls. Embellishment and ornamentation became useless.

In addition to his involvement in specifying the choice, cut, and polish of materials, Loos also paid close attention to their natural graining or patterning, arranging abstract or often anthropomorphic compositions. He liked to play with the material's materiality, its inherent qualities—as Alberti had wanted to—to excite the viewers' imagination. The critic Ludwig Hevesi claimed to have discerned the anatomical details of a muscular body moving in a magic grotto (Fig. 119).[18] The source of this remarkable facility to suggest figures from patterns in stone may be traced to Loos's early childhood in his father's yard. His mastery of marble, which has been compared to that of Mies van der Rohe, was so exceptional that the architectural community has not seen its equal for centuries.

Loos was similarly fascinated by wood, whose polished, smooth, natural surface he loved. Among his few furniture designs, the armoire for Gustav Turnowsky (Fig. 41), whose apartment he designed in 1900, is, more than just a remarkable realization, a rationalist manifesto in its own right. Loos later formulated his theory about furniture reliant on the craft of woodworking: "To attain a surface, the woodworker can assemble his wood in different ways. One of them is the frame and panel system. Between the frame and the panel is slid a fillet that makes the transition between the two, or else the frame is provided with a groove because the panel is almost always recessed. That's all. A century ago the technique was exactly the same. I am certain that nothing has changed in this domain and that all the nov-

41   GUSTAV TURNOWSKY APARTMENT: VIENNA, c. 1900.
Bedroom armoire designed by Loos.

elties extolled by the Viennese Secession and the Belgian Modernists are only aberrations.
Pure and simple construction should replace fantastic forms and vestigial ornament borrowed from past centuries. Straight lines and straight angles: this is how an artisan works
who is thinking about nothing but the finality of his work, his material and his tool."[19]

The work of Adolf Loos is best understood by examining the importance that he accorded
the honest use of pure materials, regardless of cost. He considered all materials equally
precious, and was convinced that finely crafted materials were preferable to the simple

absence of ornament; a distinction between *ornamentation* (a parasitic after-thought which upsets the constructive logic) and *decoration* (which reinforces the structural logic). As early as 1898, with his respect for truth and economy of materials, Loos formulated his theory of cladding, in the Semperian tradition: "We must work in such a way that confusion of the material clad with its cladding is impossible. That means, for example, that wood may be painted any color except one—the color of wood."[20]

This aesthetic consideration hinged on an ethical presupposition, one recognized by Viennese intellectuals at the turn of the century.

CHAPTER FOUR
INDIVIDUAL HOUSES
Principles

Adolf Loos is best known for his individual houses. Even during his lifetime, several of Loos's houses were celebrated as rationalist manifestoes, and set precedents that the Modern Movement would follow. These houses were also considered to be the epitome of a modern home. Yet in spite of his recognized importance, Loos realized only half of the projects he had completed on paper: a dozen houses, the summation of his built work. This was due, in part, to his confrontations with local building commissions in Vienna, Prague, and Geneva, who reproached him for the unusual configuration and bare exteriors of his constructions, and often rejected his proposals.

It is difficult, with Loos, to separate the built work from the projects on paper: the canonical works have been studied and documented, but others still await analysis.[1] Each composition was a step in a life-long search for the quintessential residential design. With each project, Loos reworked his palate of materials and forms, constantly and continually reformulating and refining the rapport between the interior and exterior, the building envelope and its habitation. Difference and continuity describe the whole of Loos's residential oeuvre—from the Villa Karma (1903–1906) to the Winternitz House (1931)—a series that does not always obey the laws of evolution. Loos, who was very concerned about how a building fit into its context, considered both function and site: "Not only the material, but also the architectural forms are linked to a place, to the ground and to an atmosphere."[2] His projects were client- and site-specific; they were never interchangeable. However, a typological analysis of form and structure reveals several repeated elements which ultimately constituted, despite their evolution, a permanent collection. Furthermore, one can see structural similarities between certain projects, despite their apparent differences, indicating a principle of repetition that allows a consideration of the projects as successive manifestations of a single rational approach.

Loos taught that in designing a project, one should proceed from the interior to the exterior. An exact distribution of internal space and its furnishings—appropriate to the finished building—was the point of departure for the composition. He taught his students to think volumetrically. The walls, the ceilings, the floors, and the material envelope that defined the space of daily life constituted, in his eyes, the first priority: the facade, the second.[3] But in this hierarchy of the *concept*, "second" did not signify superfluity; it merely indicated a further phase of development. On the other hand, the *perception* of the built work is formed in the opposite order: from the visible surface to the practical function, from the material structure to the internal volumes. Loos mastered this relationship in his houses as well as his monumental buildings, although he conceived the latter from the outside, considering their visible surfaces more significant (see chapter 7).

42　STEINER HOUSE: VIENNA, 1910.
View from garden. Photo: c. 1930.

43　HORNER HOUSE: VIENNA, 1912.
Photo: 1930.

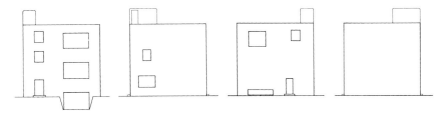

44   CUBE HOUSE DRAWINGS, 1930.
     Elevations recreated by B. Rukschcio and R. Schachel.

This analysis, which moves from perception to concept, from exterior to interior, from object to project, frees itself from Loos's teachings and examines the individual houses starting with their exterior configuration.

Most of Loos's houses, situated freely in the landscape, could develop without the boundaries of party walls. Yet they were still subject to communal regulation; clever solutions were devised to get around the constraints. In the case of the Steiner House, where Loos was allowed to build only one floor above street level, he employed a quarter-round roof to face the street, which leveled out at its apex to accommodate two more levels facing the garden, unseen from the street (Fig. 42). He used the same trick for the Horner House, both sides of which were subject to the same height limitation. In this case, a half-cylinder roof allowed the addition of one more floor (Fig. 43).

Loos's use of the cylinder was neither a formal innovation nor a break with traditional gabled roofs. Rather, this unusual configuration represented economy of space and certainty of form, demonstrating that traditions may be brushed aside, yet not betrayed, for utilitarian purposes. This was in no way an aesthetic lapse, as utility and technology were indissoluble from the ethical affirmation of forward-thinking Vienna at the beginning of the century. It was a question of linking the beauty of forms with their *raison d'être* more than with their *gestalt*. And it is by analogous reasoning that Loos made the flat roof a common feature in his urban constructions. He considered the flat concrete roof to be "the greatest architectural invention since the beginning of time,"[4] a development that even architects from past centuries would have accepted with cries of joy.[5]

Loos's houses are regular volumes in which each element, each space, and each configuration respond to the rules of composition of classical architecture.[6] The dominant volume is a massive rectangular box, sometimes approaching the ideal proportions of a cube (Rufer and Moller Houses). The latter is effectively attained in a sketch of 1930 representing a cube house of unspecified location (Fig. 44). Loos worked with a volumetric palate of sim-

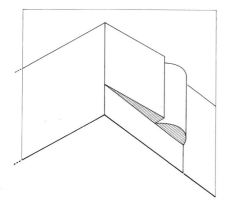

45 BAKER HOUSE: PARIS, 1927.
The right angle and the cylinder address the narrower angle of the site's context (see Figs. 82–83).

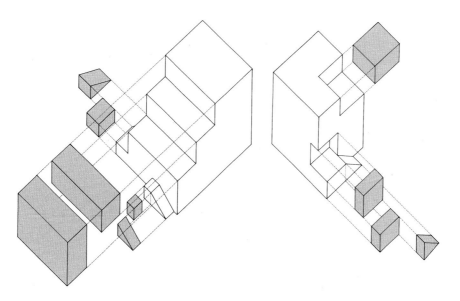

46 SCHEU AND RUFER HOUSES.
Analytical diagrams showing added and subtracted volumes of the original blocks (see Figs. 52–53, 62–67).

ple forms: cubes, rectangular boxes, and cylinders. He objected to acute angles, and if impossible to avoid—because of site shape and context—the offending angle was lost once the composition rose above the ground floor. Such was the case for the Josephine Baker House, whose site fell at the 80-degree intersection of two streets. Although he acknowledged the acute angle at street level, on the second floor Loos returned to a 90-degree angle and smoothed the wall into a half cylinder to preserve the continuity of the urban fabric (Fig. 45). Of course, this cylinder also fit perfectly into the internal organization of the house (Figs. 82–83).

Loos manipulated other smaller volumes in complex volumetric puzzles to determine the internal organization of his buildings (Fig. 46). Often, these volumes protruded from the main block, allowing for the creation of terraces—one of Loos's leitmotifs. Even his flat roofs were sometimes accessible for sheltered sunbathing (Moïssi House, Figs. 92–93). Loos felt that if it was agreeable to step out onto a terrace from one's bedroom, and if it was possible to construct this terrace because of new techniques in reinforced concrete, why should one be deprived of this pleasure, only to respect conventional forms, themselves dependent on outdated techniques? Thus, the houses were often stepped gradually, vaguely evoking the form of ancient ziggurats (Fig. 62). The Scheu House, whose form was the result of a series of rational geometric exercises, accurately represents Loos's critical relationship with tradition: an active memory of past forms combined with the possibilities of new construction methods.

In some of Loos's houses, severe blocks project out over the main entrance (Fig. 75). Although somewhat threatening, these extrusions helped a house to gain intimacy: the projections created niches and alcoves below and private terraces above. Inversely, other houses featured subtractive volumes. The space above the recess became a balcony (Figs. 69, 79b), and if the recess opened onto the building's plinth, it formed a portico (Figs. 87–88). In the Steiner House (Fig. 60) or in the the project for the Villa Konstandt (Fig. 85), the recess between the two wings rises all the way to the roof—forming a classical tripartite facade.

Whatever spatial manipulations were made, Loos's houses remain immutably compact. Given the apparent thickness of their walls, the houses seem incapable of successfully accommodating life's daily activities. In addition, the distribution of windows consistently misrepresents the interior layout, and access stairs and their landings are attached to the outside of the blocks. One must cross the threshold and pass through the exterior envelope to comprehend the coherent intricacies of the interiors. Needless to say, Loos did not subscribe to the transparency of the glass architecture of the Modern Movement.

Loos's walls were rough-cast; he considered stucco to be a cladding consistent with the character of Viennese architecture, but condemned its use as an imitation of an expensive material such as stone. He espoused the realistic portrayal of stucco as a skin—a protective coating covering a wall of bricks—in the tradition of "the good old Viennese stucco."

64

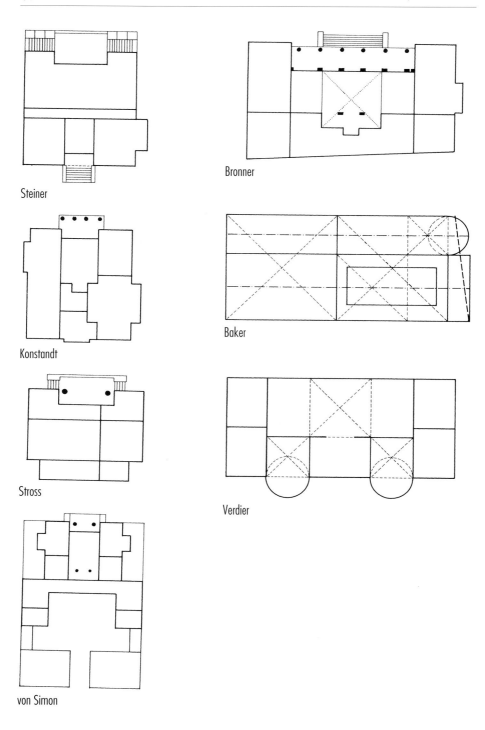

Steiner

Bronner

Konstandt

Baker

Stross

Verdier

von Simon

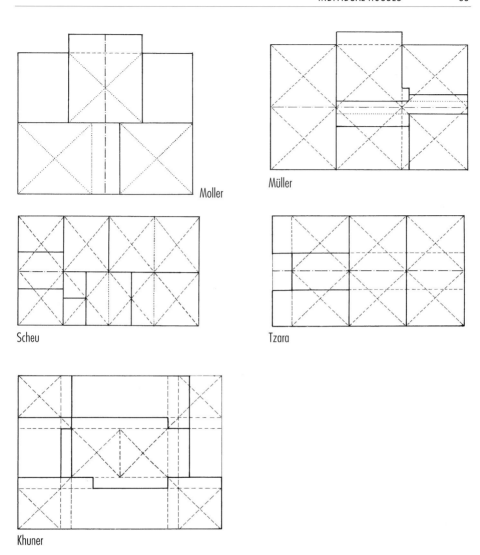

Moller

Müller

Scheu

Tzara

Khuner

47   SCHEMATIC DIAGRAMS: TWELVE HOUSES BY LOOS.
     The classical references and geometric organization of the plans indicates the use of a regulating system.

Consequently, the exterior surfaces of Loos's houses were smooth, white, and without ornament. This choice explained neither a refutation of the past nor the desire for a new aesthetic, but a respect for the local tradition and the nature of the material. It was equally an
ethical choice and a radical criticism of contemporary misrepresentation.[7] The neutrality of
Loos's facades and the absence of ornament may have been simple, but were far from simplistic: "This stripping," wrote Loos, "acts like a new charm and exercises a stimulating
effect. The windmill that does not make noise wakens the miller."[8]

Loos concentrated his efforts principally on the shapes of forms and the articulation of
solids and voids. This preoccupation is apparent in his facades, but is also implicit in the
volumetric composition and necessarily depends on the organization of the plans. Loos
drew his principles of composition from the tradition of German classicism (that of Karl
Friedrich Schinkel, himself influenced by the Italian Renaissance and Greco-Roman
antiquity). The formal aspects of his plans and facades (Figs. 84–89) testify to the perma-
nence of his "villas" in their Palladian sense: "Ever since humanity became imbued with
the grandeur of classical antiquity," wrote Loos about his school's teaching methods, "the
masters of construction have united in a common thought....It is this thought with which I
want to inculcate my students. Today is built on yesterday, as yesterday is built on the day
before."[9]

The pursuit of geometrically harmonic proportion, axial symmetry, classical purity, and
simplicity of form play a determining role in Loos's creations. In the nineteenth century,
the use of regulating lines was common practice for architecture students: a simple method
of projection, devoid of original content. An analysis of several of Loos's plans and facades
allows one to ascertain that he did use these rules of composition (Fig. 47). The original
facade of the Tzara House (Fig. 48) shows that the golden section was used to determine
the height and to subdivide it into two unequal surfaces: the upper white rough-cast square
and the pieced stone rectangle that forms the base. The partially erased lines of this sketch
can still be seen on the tracing of the previous scheme.

Loos's volumes and facades obey the laws of symmetry (Figs. 60, 69, 75, 87, 88, 91),
with a regular succession of square and rectangular windows. He was remarkably persistent
in his use of the classical language in an era when the avant-garde championed asymmetry.
With his facades, Loos affirmed and even flaunted his right to be out of fashion.

However, the symmetry of Loos's exteriors are sometimes upset by the requirements of
the interior layout. Consequently, asymmetries and partial deformations coexist in his most
rigorous plans. The facades undergo compositional manipulations to emphasize comple-
mentary axes, geometric tracings, or simply the dynamism of intersecting forms. In the
Rufer House, for example, Loos studied the division of solids and voids in four sketches to
develop the interior spaces (Fig. 49a). Yet for the exterior, his motivations were less prag-
matic: he set a copy of a long frieze from the Parthenon in the rough-cast stone of the wall.

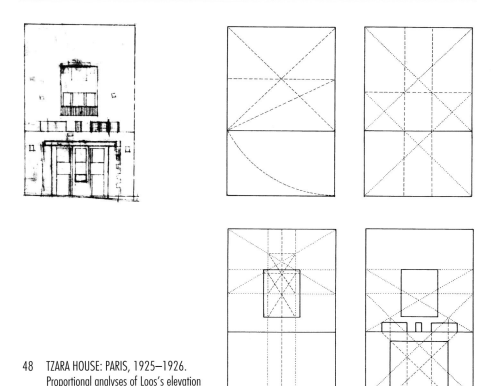

48 TZARA HOUSE: PARIS, 1925–1926.
Proportional analyses of Loos's elevation
(see Fig. 69).

(Fig. 64), as much to accentuate the deeply classical character of the house as to balance the composition. Loos, recognizing the timelessness of classicism, realized that he could make classical references without being bound by classical rules. He simply followed his typically unerring instincts. Each project developed along two separate paths: the articulated expansion of the interior and the refined classicism of the exterior were worked individually, as far as possible, and then met quite late in the design process for whatever minor adjustments were necessary.

Loos's fenestration tends to be subdivided into small squares or rectangles which obey a modular system (Fig. 50). This system, of course, corresponds to the overall geometry of the facade (Steiner, Figs. 59–60 and Scheu Houses, Figs. 62–63). In general, the living room is connected to an open terrace with access to the garden. In certain projects, a classical portico completes the ensemble and marks the passage from enclosed space to enclosed nature (Figs. 85, 88). This designed descent to nature on the garden side contrasts with the progression on the street side; passage between private and public domains is restrained, neutral

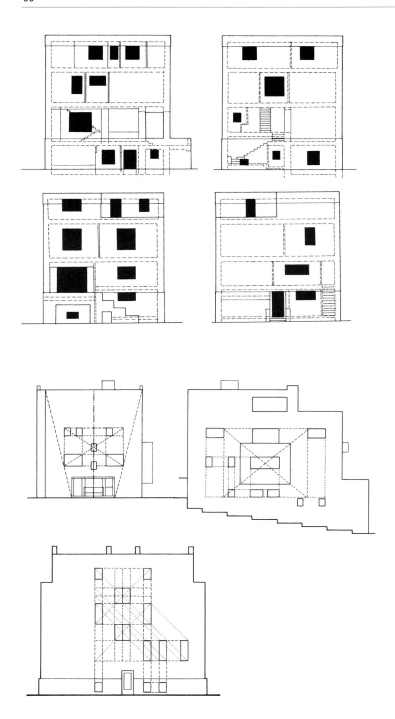

50 WINDOW TYPOLOGY.
Clockwise from top left: Scheu, Tzara, Winternitz, Bronner.

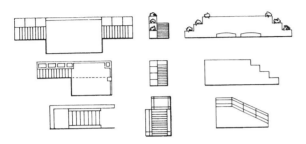

51 GARDEN STAIR TYPOLOGY.
Top to bottom: Steiner, Rufer, Scheu.

and unobtrusive. A few bare steps lead to the front door; their role is purely functional. Yet the stairs that link house and garden are deliberate and imposing; two monumental and symmetrical flights play an important role in the composition of the facade (Fig. 51).

Since the 1920s, critics have celebrated Loos's radical suppression of ornament and stripping of facades as the indisputable expressions of his modernity. However, Loos was not whole-heartedly supported by the Modern Movement. Even if one disregards his blatantly "decorative" organization of elements on the facade (shapes, windows, stairs), one cannot ignore the introduction, in certain houses, of entirely "ornamental" features which reveal the classical language of architecture. In various projects, Loos employed cornices, friezes of mouldings and garlands, porticos (distyle, tetrastyle or hexastyle with Tuscan or

opposite page:

49a RUFER HOUSE: VIENNA 1922.
Disposition of windows on "transparent" elevations (drawings reconstructed from sketch by Loos).

49b VILLA MÜLLER: PRAGUE, 1928–1930 (TOP), AND VILLA WINTERNITZ: PRAGUE, 1931–1932 (BOTTOM).
Geometry of elevations.

Ionic orders), caryatids (to support a covered porch), and rusticated stonework. As non-structural elements and references to ancient architecture, these elements enlarge the semantic field of Loos's deliberately "laconic" compositions; they testify in his eyes to the legitimacy and to the almost "natural" character of classical ornament[10]—that which is comparable to grammar. "It disciplines us, and with us, our forms; in spite of the ethnic and linguistic differences, it engenders a community of forms and artistic concepts."[11] And it is with the study of classical ornament that Loos started the course on drawing at his school of architecture—a study which was then expanded to include analysis of the orders and mouldings.[12]

However, one must note that Loos used classical ornament openly in a small number of unrealized projects (Villas Konstandt, Figs. 84–86; Bronner, Fig. 87; Stross, Fig. 88; and von Simon, Fig. 89) and only one built work (the Rufer House, Fig. 64). This restricted group should be distinguished from the whole of the urban houses where Loos, while still relying on classical proportions, did not use ornament.

Adolf Loos criticized and objected to the convention of disguising a mediocre house (and perhaps average occupants) with a glorious facade (the "Potemkin villa"; see chapter 1). On the exterior, Loos's houses presented severe surfaces, "without character," which portrayed only the purity and clarity of ethical and aesthetic order. Meanwhile, these anonymous exteriors housed innumerable details, sensitively designed to accommodate the inhabitants' personalities: "we should build in a style, just as our fathers had done, which shuts out the outer world," he wrote. "The house should be discrete on the outside; its entire richness should be disclosed on the inside."[13]

Loos designed each house according to the specific demands and desires of his clients, who often were or became his friends. Their social position or their social aspirations were reflected in both the layout of the plans and in the facades. Fairly similar in appearance and even in their interior organization, the Moller House (Figs. 74–78) and the Villa Müller (Figs. 79–81) still each conveyed the distinct personalities of their occupants.

The implications of room size and configuration were the basis for the Raumplan (the resolution of the plan in space), the term used to define and explain the Loosian method of design.[14] For Loos, space was not to be treated as surface but as volume. Towards this end, he would determine the size and positioning of volumes by analyzing their use requirements. The overall volume was then enriched by the overlap of these spaces. Towards the end of his life, he would admit that the "solution to the problem of the distribution of the living spaces, in space and not in surface...floor by floor," was "the great architectural revolution" of the modern era.[15] The interior of the house became a puzzle of interlocking volumes disposed on several levels and connected by several flights of stairs. Were it built, the Villa Konstandt (Figs. 84–86) would have been the most articulated example of this

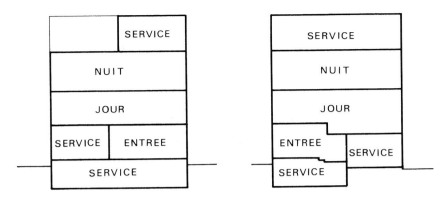

52 RUFER HOUSE: VIENNA, 1922.
Internal use diagrams (see Fig. 66).

method: Loos designed the project with fourteen levels in all—five constituted the living zone, and they were connected by eight staircases. Even the attic occupied multiple levels.

Loos's houses are divided into two zones: the served space and the serving space. The served space is reserved for the masters' and their friends' activities. It is the home proper, which is then further subdivided into public (diurnal) and private (nocturnal) areas. "The man that possesses his own house lives on two levels. He rigorously separates his life into two parts. Into daily life and nocturnal life. Living and sleeping....In the morning all the members of the family come down to the ground floor at the same time. The baby too is brought down and spends the day with its mother in the living spaces."[16] The second zone, the serving space, groups the necessary services so that the household may be run smoothly. Serving space extends over and under served space (Fig. 52).

For Loos, the way one entered a house was of the greatest importance. The entrance could not be merely a door into a hall; it had to function as a zone of purification where one could disencumber oneself of the outside world and public life. Therefore, the entrance becomes a sequential event, with a cloakroom to discard one's city clothes, a small room with a toilet, and a reception vestibule, sometimes furnished with a wash basin (Fig. 53) so one could literally wash one's hands of the outside world before ascending a narrow stair to enter the sanctum of the home.

The entrance progression led to a vast and continuous floor that linked, in a complex chain of interlocking volumes of variegated heights, the living room, the dining room, the library, and often the music room (Fig. 54). Ideally, this ensemble was oriented towards the garden and culminated in a balcony or terrace. This multifunctional daytime continuum was the focus of family life, a vital space in which one could both cultivate the spirit and

53   RUFER HOUSE: VIENNA, 1922.
      Entrance hall. Photo: 1930.

nourish the body. The topmost level of the house was the place for intimacy and rest where the bedrooms, the bathroom, and sometimes a playroom for the children were found.

In Loos's houses, the serving spaces were similarly divided into two groups. The first was situated on the ground floor near the main entrance and extended to the basement. It grouped the kitchen, the storeroom, the wine cellar, the central heating, the fuel room, the watchman's room (if applicable), the garage, and other auxiliary rooms. The second part of the serving space occupied the top floor under the roof: the servants' quarters, the laundry room, and other service rooms. This division of functions was not immutable, but the hierarchy that it implied was generally respected and adapted to the specifics of each project.

The internal organization of Loos's houses, specifically the overlapping of levels and vertical circulation, owed much to modern materials, construction, and inventions (reinforced concrete and electricity). New technology enabled him to create rooms overlooking rooms (the overhanging "cafe" of the Baker House, Fig. 83), or to project a bay window from the facade (the Moller House, Fig. 75), while respecting the budgetary constraints of the project. Electricity allowed the introduction of elevators and dumbwaiters: vertical communi-

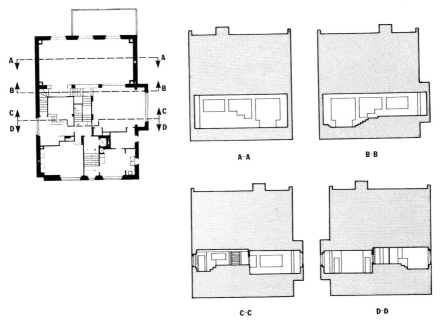

54 VILLA MÜLLER: PRAGUE, 1928–1930.
Four sections through sitting room. Drawings by B. Podrecca (see Fig. 80).

cation became just as easy as horizontal (Figs. 80, 87). The kitchen, with its odors, could be concealed under the dining room in the serving zone so that the functioning of the home became virtually invisible and undetectable. The advent of central heating and electric appliances (the Moller House) also contributed to the comfort of the inhabitants. The garage proved indispensable: even at the beginning of the century, the automobile was an essential part of a truly modern lifestyle.

For Loos, a predetermined ground plane had no particular correlation to the supple and autonomous division of the interior. He contrasted heavy, static, supporting exterior walls in brick or ashlar with lighter interior partitions; thin wood paneling or plaster that permitted more flexible subdivision. Similarly, he juxtaposed the sobriety of the stucco exterior with interior cladding of rare marble and highly polished woods. The joinery of these materials—evocatively paired, book-matched slabs—constitutes the essence of Loos's interior decoration. He also showed extreme skill in his use of light, filtering in natural light from above, the side, across the paneling, or simply allowing it to pour in freely (Villas Karma and Müller).

Loos used cladding materials to characterize and define spaces. He typically used plaster walls and exposed brick fireplaces in the living areas, he turned residual space into functional storage, and he preconfigured space with built-in furniture. He believed that the task of truly modern architecture was to construct houses where the furniture (except tables and chairs) could be integrated with the walls.

Despite his interest in creating very specifically designed environments, Loos generally avoided designing free-standing furniture. He believed that a home had to agree with the style of the occupants, and allowed their choice of furniture to help personalize each house. He compared the room with a violin: "It adapts to the people who live in it, like a violin adapts to the music."[17] He preferred to send his clients to craftsmen known for their respect for tradition. Concerning standard objects—chairs and tableware—he thought, as explained in chapter three, that centuries of use had already decided their shape. There was no reason to replace a Chippendale chair, except by a Thonet chair, to save a little money.

This search for durable, classical, and traditional objects was inherent to Loos's concept of the house as a conservative entity rather than as a work of art. He believed that housing ought to strive to free itself from the transient wiles of fashion, and should rely on a more permanent and dependable style. Paul Khuner wrote Loos in 1927, thanking him for a second time for the 1907 renovation of his Viennese apartment. During the last twenty years, he explained, all his friends had been obliged to renovate their houses three or four times, while he always felt at ease in his own apartment.[18] Two years later, Khuner, testifying again to his confidence in Loos's principles and sensibilities, commissioned him to design a country house near Payerbach. An exquisite creation, the Khuner House became famous.

Houses

Loos's rational aesthetic was derived from his realism, but he never established or limited himself to a single immutable system. His houses, despite their compositional similarities or references, could be neither classified as types nor labeled unique. Loos's beliefs evolved with each project: "Man cannot repeat an achievement," he said. "He is created anew each day and the new human being is incapable of producing that which the old one created."[19]

Irreducible as Loos's oeuvre may seem, the houses can be grouped into two series: urban work, which tend to be more classical, and rural. This categorization is liberal enough to accommodate the evolution, overlap, and contradiction within and between the two groups. For Loos, whose only dogma was the refusal of all dogma, a break with his own principles was not necessarily permanent or meaning-laden, it was merely a bending of practical necessities when the latter required transformations and transgressions.

The Villa Karma (Clarens, near Montreux, 1903–1906; Figs. 55–58) was Loos's first house and one of his greatest works. It was built on Lake Geneva for Theodore Beer, a psychiatry professor on the medical faculty in Vienna. Loos preserved the original foundations and the rectangular structure of the traditional "master's house," and designed a new structure with respect for its surroundings in both form and material. As he wrote later, in 1910: "There were a lot of stones on the banks and since the former inhabitants had built all their houses with stones, I wanted to do as they had. Because first, this solution is less expensive...and second, the delivery of material is less trouble."[20]

This attention to the local context testifies both to Loos's rationality and to his understanding of traditional construction (stripped of the picturesque). At one point, the Swiss authorities thought they should interfere in the villa's construction because they found it "much too simple" to face the natural beauty of the lake. In 1906, Loos, after a disagreement with Beer, abandoned the project. The villa was finished by Hugo Ehrlich in 1912. Although the extent of the modifications made by this architect is unclear, he was closer to Hoffmann and the Secession in style. But Loos's hand is evident in several rooms—in their refinement, their semi-precious materials, and their seductively sculpted concavity (Figs. 57–58).

The Steiner, Scheu, Rufer, Tzara, and Moller Houses and the Villa Müller, built in three European capitals, were for nearly fifty years the best-known examples of Loos's architecture. Their stripped facades were rapidly assimilated into the formal purism of the 1920s, despite historical references which were dismissed as insignificant sentimentality. The house Loos designed for Hugo and Lilly Steiner (Vienna, 1910, Figs. 42, 59–61) became one of the obligatory precedents for architects in the 1920s and 1930s. The photograph of its

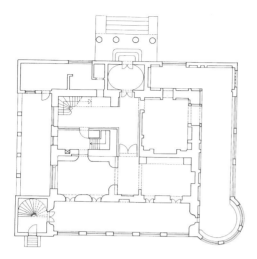

55 VILLA KARMA: CLARENS (NEAR MONTREUX), 1903–1906.
    Plan.

56 VILLA KARMA.
    View from garden. Photo: c. 1963.

57   VILLA KARMA.
Dining room. Photo: 1930.

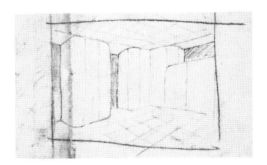

58   VILLA KARMA.
Sketch of dining room.

above and on opposite page:

59   STEINER HOUSE: VIENNA, 1910.
      Elevations, sections, and plan.

garden facade (Fig. 60) was reproduced in almost all the literature of the Modern Movement as an incontestable example of revolutionary radicalism. Its originality—the simple geometry of the volumes, the smooth white walls, the flat roof, the frameless openings—was judged to express the refusal of historicism. Yet its somewhat Palladian classicism—its tripartite symmetry, axial plan, compositional purity, stripped down facade, and utilitarian simplicity—was ignored. Ironically, the innovative character of the Steiner House was not derived from a desire to negate history, but, as always with Loos, from the desire to renew classical tradition.

The basic interior organization of Loos's houses was present even in this early building. The living area, raised slightly above ground level, was separated from the more private area (bedrooms, Lilly Steiner's painting studio) on the first floor. Served space was clearly separated from serving space; it was neatly tucked away in the basement and attic. A pared-down exterior and a refined interior: classicism married to Anglo-Saxon domesticity

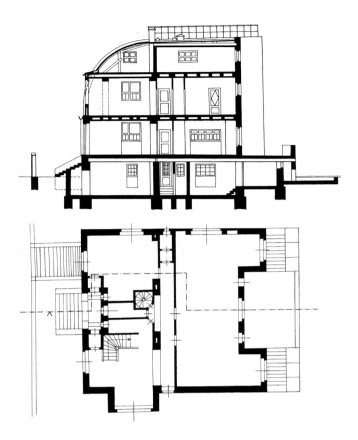

in a search for spatial continuity. The large rectangular room on the ground floor was at the same time the living room, the dining room, and the music room, and was an early example of the linked spaces which became a distinctively Loosian trait. A centrifugal force seems to have spiralled the furniture for eating and conversing around an open area, adjacent to a terrace leading to the garden. Draperies allowed the division of this spatial "continuum," which, in its intentions, resembled the goals of Frank Lloyd Wright.

Dr. Gustav and Helen Scheu's house (Vienna, 1912–1913, Figs. 62–63) was probably the first—and certainly the purist—European example of a flat roof used as an outdoor terrace. The stepped form of the Scheu House was a prototype; it played an important role in the development of early twentieth-century architecture, in a time when the merits of flat roofs were widely debated. Its ziggurat shape challenged the roofing idea of local tradition: "[The Scheu House] has raised general disapproval," Loos wrote in 1923, "We thought that this

60   STEINER HOUSE.
     View from garden. Photo: c. 1930.

61   STEINER HOUSE.
     View from street. Photo: c. 1930.

type of building would be beautiful in Algeria, but not in Vienna. I was not thinking about the Orient when I built this house. I only thought it would be nice to walk out onto a large terrace from the bedrooms on the first floor. In Vienna as in Algeria. Thus this terrace repeated at the second floor—a rented apartment—represented something uncommon and abnormal. Someone went to the municipal council to ask if this type of building was permitted by law."[21]

Construction was interrupted in 1912: municipal authorities feared for the aesthetic tranquility of the Hietzing quarter.[22] However, the sole conciliatory gesture Loos made was to attach ivy to the length of the garden side to make the facade less austere.

Despite the elaborate composition of the fenestration, which was attuned to the stepped tiers, the exterior of the Scheu House was considered shocking in that it revealed a world "without qualities." It disturbed the accepted sensibilities, asserting its rationalist, polemical architecture of both memory and innovation, rejecting Art Nouveau and the picturesque.[23] With the Scheu House, the flat roof, an ancient form, redefined itself with the innovations of new construction and new materials: "The choice of a flat roof, which is the most beautiful, the least expensive and the most durable of roofs, is the criterion which lets one know if we are dealing with an architect or stage designer."[24]

In the Scheu House, the gathering and reception spaces (living room, music room, library, dining room) were grouped on the slightly raised ground floor, the bedrooms were on the first floor, and the serving spaces—with the exception of the kitchen—were in the semi-basement. The second floor was a rental apartment, completely independent from the rest of the house. Loos used dark, unpolished oak in the day area and white, painted wood in the bedrooms. Ornamental wood beams spanned the ceiling of the reception rooms, and Loos's recommended furnishings also helped evoke a Richardsonian atmosphere. The great success of the Scheu House is due almost certainly to the progressive sensibilities of Mr. Scheu, a lawyer and Viennese intellectual aligned with the Garden City Movement, and close enough to the architect to understand and approve of his rational choices.

The Raumplan made its first definitive appearance in the house of Joseph and Marie Rufer (Vienna, 1922; Figs. 52–53, 64–67). The building was a cubic volume: four bearing walls defined a space of 10 x 10 meters, or 33 x 33 feet. At the center, a column functioned both as a duct for the gas-fueled central heating system and as a conduit for water and electricity. The heart of the house was a series of interwoven spaces on the first floor combining, on two levels, the living room, the music room, the library, the dining room, and a terrace leading out to the garden. For the first time, the kitchen was placed *below* the daily activities zone.

Seen from the street, the surfaces of the Rufer House were completely bare, even the windows stripped of trim. To determine their placement, Loos balanced the black of the

62   SCHEU HOUSE: VIENNA, 1912–1913.
View from garden. Photo: 1930.

openings with the white of the walls on his elevations, also considering the organization of the interior (Fig. 49a). The volume was capped by a blank frieze and an antique cornice (Fig. 65). A Parthenon frieze was positioned low on the street facade. An ornament, a fragment of a classical work, it balanced the purist abstraction of the cube. It also inscribed the house and its architecture into a history.

The house built for Tristan Tzara in the Montmartre section of Paris, 1925–26 (Figs. 68–73), owes its renown principally to its illustrious owner. Tzara's connection with the avant-garde has both colored and overshadowed any in-depth analysis of the work, which is far from a Dada manifesto. With its symmetrical facade and its relatively conservative interior, it testifies to the ties which bound Loos to the classical tradition.

The ground floor of the Tzara House was occupied by a rental apartment. Initially the house was to be four stories high, but per Tzara's wishes, the top story was never built. This decision caused a deformation of the original conception of the facade as a white square on a brown ashlar stone base (Fig. 69), forming a rectangle based on the proportions of the

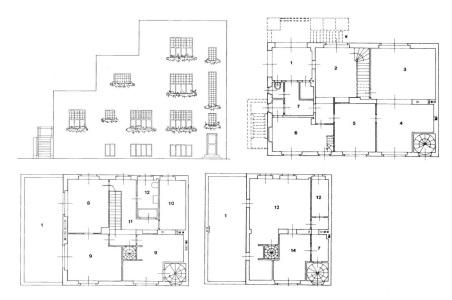

63 SCHEU HOUSE.

Street elevation and ground floor, first floor, and second floor plans.
1. terrace; 2. sitting room; 3. music room/office; 4. library; 5. dining room; 6. kitchen; 7. entrance hall;
8. child's bedroom; 9. bedroom; 10. maid's bedroom; 11. hall; 12. bathroom; 13. winter garden;
14. master bedroom.

golden section (Fig. 48). All the formal elements of this facade, from the recessed bays to the deliberately positioned gutters, fell symmetrically, respecting the harmony of the golden section. Jay Hambridge has proposed that the lower recessed balcony was cut into the stone to resemble an Egyptian tomb (Fig. 48).[25] Perhaps inspired by Tzara, Loos may have repeated this form in the upper part of the facade, behind which were housed the spaces of life and creation, thereby creating a link with eternity. Loos and Tzara both admired primitive cultures; Tzara collected African objects and surrealist paintings by Arp and Max Ernst. The house owed its form to their works.

The interior spaces were distributed hierarchically according to a tripartite division reflecting the organization of the facade (Fig. 68, plan). The volumes were separated by several different types of staircases (Fig. 68, section), which can be seen either as links or breaks in the spatial continuum (Fig. 71). Loos was a master at the art of playing on the difficulties of the site; the flexibility of the Raumplan allowed him to build on sloped or uneven land.

64 RUFER HOUSE: VIENNA, 1922.
View from street, showing Parthenon frieze.
Photo: 1930.

65 RUFER HOUSE.
Detail of street elevation. Photo: 1986.

66   RUFER HOUSE.
Plans and sections.

67   RUFER HOUSE.
Music room, sitting room, and entrance stair with steps leading to dining room. Second floor accessed by return stair. Photo: 1930.

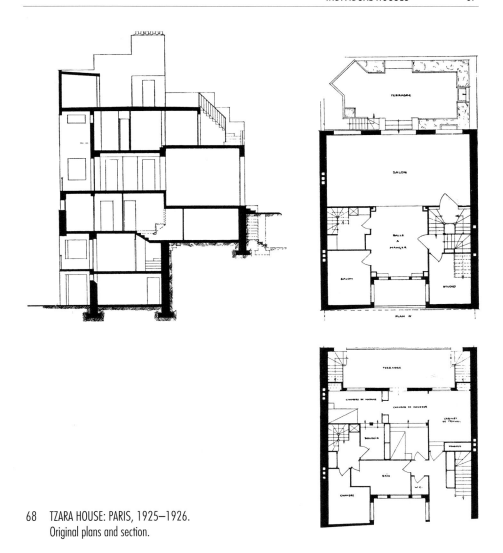

68   TZARA HOUSE: PARIS, 1925–1926.
      Original plans and section.

The house built for Hans and Anny Moller (Vienna, 1927–1928, Figs. 74–78) is generally considered the culmination of Loos's long intellectual voyage. The house was a simple composition of basic geometric volumes. On the street side it presented a nearly square symmetrical facade with a projected box above the entry. The box became a balcony on the second floor. The garden facade was extremely simple, attaining an unprecedented modicum of architectural expression. All the elements—windows, balcony, terrace, railings, stair—were exclusively functional and entirely devoid of decorative elements. The interior

clockwise from top left:

69a TZARA HOUSE.
Facade by Adolf Loos. Photomontage: 1930. Top
floor—two bedrooms and a bathroom—had not yet
been constructed.

69b TZARA HOUSE.
Photo: 1930.

70 TZARA HOUSE.
View from court. Photo: c. 1930.

71 TZARA HOUSE.
Sitting room and raised dining room (at left). Photo: c. 1930.

72 TZARA HOUSE.

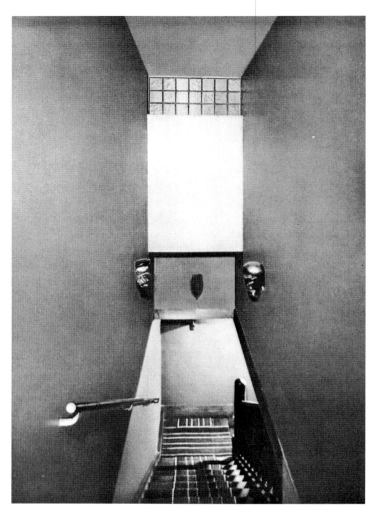

73 TZARA HOUSE.
Entrance stair. Photo: 1930.

opposite page:

74 MOLLER HOUSE: VIENNA, 1927–1928.
View from garden. Photo: c. 1929.

75 MOLLER HOUSE.
View from street. Photo: 1962.

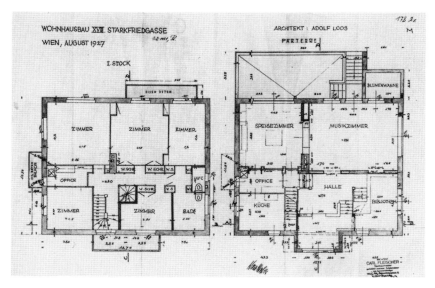

WOHNHAUSBAU XVII. STARKFRIEDGASSE
WIEN, AUGUST 1927

ARCHITEKT : ADOLF LOOS

76   MOLLER HOUSE.
Plans—*zimmer:* bedroom; *speisezimmer:* dining room; *musikzimmer:* music room; *halle:* living room;
küche: kitchen; *bad:* bathroom; *blumenwanne:* greenhouse.

organization was born of the simple application of the principles of the Raumplan. The entrance hall prompted a clean stop prior to entering the sanctity of the purified environment; one passes through to the living area, which combined the music room, the library, and the dining room. The five bedrooms were on the floor above. The serving spaces, clearly separated from the served spaces, were in the basement, the ground floor, and the top floor. The only movable furniture in the house were the tables and Thonet chairs; the rest was built into the structure. The interior of the Moller House owes its celebrity to its materials. In the dining room, travertine columns emerged from Gaboon plywood paneling (Fig. 78), and the somber paneling in the music room and its matte-brown, black-veined ebony parquet created a warm, harmonious atmosphere. This room is known for its acoustics, to which Loos paid particular attention.

Like the Moller House, the exterior of the villa for the engineer Frantisek Müller and his wife (Prague, 1928–1930, Figs. 79–81) was also cubic, white, and pared-down, and its side facade had a suspended projection (Fig. 79a). Its entrance led to Loos's requisite vestibule with a small room with a toilet. The living area was reached by a sort of trick stair: one had to ascend and then descend two sets of four steps before arriving at the living room at the end of a hall. Six steps led to the latter, and then two more up to the dining room. This difference

77   MOLLER HOUSE.
Dining room from music room. Photo: 1930.

78   MOLLER HOUSE.
Music room from dining room. Photo: 1930.

79a VILLA MÜLLER: PRAGUE, 1928–1930.
Side elevation.

of level was the only separation between the two spaces. Another eight steps up from the living room was Mrs. Müller's boudoir. From there, four steps led down to Mr. Müller's library. The boudoir itself was divided in two, housing both an intimate corner niche with an oblong window onto the living room, and a more spacious corner for writing, three steps further down, from which one could descend directly into the living room. Mr. Müller's library was the only space that was at once on the same level as the rest of the diurnal spaces, but that was isolated and protected from their activity. The bedrooms were on the upper story, which could be reached by either a straightforward switch-back stair, or by elevator.

The materials were chosen to express the elegance and simplicity of the house itself. The cipolin, a green marble from Siena, veined with red and yellow, clad the stair wall and the columns in the living room. The white walls, the red bricks of the chimney, the yellow draperies, and the large, predominantly blue carpet completed the atmosphere. The dining room and library were paneled in mahogany, and the boudoir, in clear lemon wood. Adolf

79b VILLA MÜLLER.
Street elevation. Photo: 1930.

Loos celebrated his sixtieth birthday in this impressive house, considered by many to be his masterpiece.

The theoretical project (it was unsolicited and was never built) for Josephine Baker (Paris, 1927; Figs. 82–83) was of a unique approach. Loos cleverly manipulated the building's oblong form to comply with the peculiar site. While the ground floor respected the lines of the street (an acute angle), the two upper floors were liberated from this unwanted, impure form. The right angle replaced the acute angle, and the mass of the building became an overhang above the sidewalk (Fig. 45). A skewed cylinder recaptured the original deformation to balance the composition with the site and the neighboring buildings. The compactness of the volume, the flat roof, the small, low openings, the vast blind surfaces, and the bands of black and white marble created an exotic and mysterious image, vaguely evocative of African architecture, while providing no clues as to the interior.

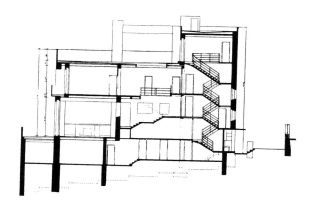

80 VILLA MÜLLER.
    Plans and section—1. basement; 2. garage; 3. chauffeur; 4 & 5. laundry; 6. boiler; 7. entrance hall;
    8. antechamber; 9. small office; 10. living room; 11. dining room; 12. office; 13. kitchen; 14. library;
    15. boudoir; 16. bedroom; 17. man's dressing room; 18. woman's dressing room; 19. child's bedroom;
    20. guest room; 21. maid's bedroom.

81a VILLA MÜLLER.
Reading niche in boudoir with window onto sitting room.

81b   VILLA MÜLLER.
Sitting room. One arrives by stair, and must climb another eight steps to the dining room, from which one overlooks the sitting room. Loos often used a difference in level as the sole method of spatial differentiation (see Figs. 71, 77, 78). Photo: 1930.

The interior was organized around a glass-walled swimming pool accessible from the second floor. The spacious entry of the house led to the first floor, to a spectacular reception area overlooking the swimming pool. Two corridors linked the large salon, reserved for social events, with the smaller, more intimate salon, itself lengthened by the cylindrical "cafe." Four long windows in the corridors and in the small salon allowed observation of the swimmers. The reception area stretched to the upper floor and was reached by a semi-circular metal staircase. The bedrooms, the access platform to the pool, and the dining room were contiguous (the latter separated from the kitchen by two floors). Two elevators eased vertical communication and circulation, as all the serving spaces were grouped on the ground floor and in the basement. In this complex and seductive house for Josephine Baker, the Raumplan was enriched by unusually erotic spatial manipulations, and the project paid homage to the era's glitterati, described by Arthur Schnitzler in *Traumnovelle*.[26]

Like the project for Josephine Baker, the Konstandt, Bronner, Stross, and von Simon villas were designed for an urban context, but were never built. Certain compositional analogies in their proposed siting justifies their grouping: their exterior configurations were explicitly

82   BAKER HOUSE: PARIS, 1927.
      Model.

classical, as much for the organization of volumes as for the use of porticos and decorative elements. However, the arrangement of their interiors resulted from a skillful application of the Raumplan allied with modern construction.

Loos designed the villa for H. Konstandt (Olmutz, 1919; Figs. 84–86) in collaboration with his student Paul Engelmann, who later worked on a house for Wittgenstein.[27] The Villa Konstandt was a rectangular prism with projecting bays, borrowing the essence of the tripartite plan of the Steiner House (Fig. 86). Its symmetry also determined the garden facade (Fig. 85); entrance to this side of the house was through an Ionic portico topped by a balcony whose balustrade was the sculpted frieze of the entablature. Another balcony on the street side was a liberal interpretation of the caryatids of the Erechtheion; large female figures adorned the columns of the portico, standing on and holding up two processional friezes (Fig. 84). Above the upper frieze was a cornice decorated with garlands. It capped the steep-roofed building (Fig. 85). The arrangement of the window openings and the rusti-cated base reinforced the villa's classical appearance, in complete contradiction with descriptions of Loos's "style" that one reads in histories of modern architecture.

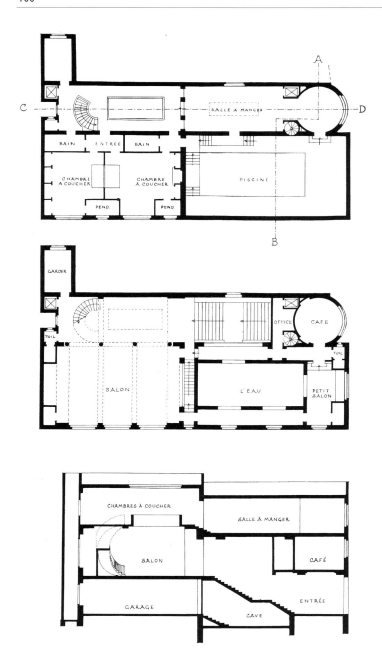

83   BAKER HOUSE.
Plans and section drawings by L. Bakalowits.

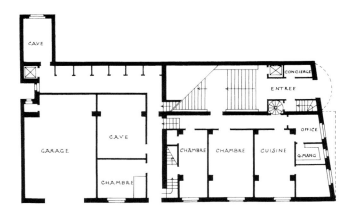

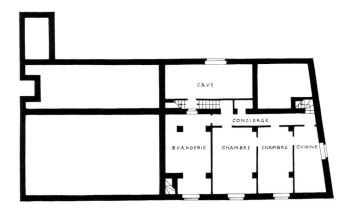

84   VILLA KONSTANDT: OLMÜTZ, 1919.
      Northeast (street) elevation. Note quotation of Erechtheion caryatids.

The interior developed on several levels, consistent with the hierarchical organization found in Loos's urban houses. The dining room was on the raised ground floor, and was connected to the kitchen by dumbwaiter. The interlocking spaces and shifting axes indicate a complexity of plan, in contrast to the formal unity of the facades.

In his project for a villa for Samuel Bronner (Vienna, 1921; Fig. 87), Loos employed his usual palate of external elements: bays, niches, terraces, stairs, decoration, and carefully distributed windows. But the villa was distinguished by its monumental garden portico, for which Loos made many sketches, vacillating between unfluted Ionic columns and fluted Doric columns, ultimately deciding on unfluted Doric. Governed by the Raumplan, the interior was organized around two axes and seemed to be, with its main hall of strongly articulated recessed spaces, the inverse of the extrusions on the exterior. The living and reception rooms occupied a large area on the ground floor. As in the Villa Konstandt, the bedrooms on the upper floor opened onto a balcony above the portico. An elevator assured easy circulation between the five stories of the villa; it was to have been built in a neighborhood of houses of comparable height and luxury.

The same contrast or inconsistency between facade and plan appeared in the project for the Villa Stross (1922, Fig. 88). Its exterior, characterized by a symmetry of volumes and openings as well as by a colossal Ionic portico on the garden side, was in marked contrast to the disposition of the complex, hierarchical interior, where practicality and inhabitability reigned. In this little-known project, Loos enclosed a modern plan, a "machine for living," in an equally modern envelope (built by modern construction methods) and then sheathed the whole in a traditional "epidermis."

85   VILLA KONSTANDT.

Southeast (garden) elevation drawing by Paul Engelmann.

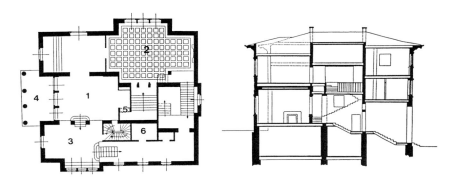

86   VILLA KONSTANDT.

Plan of diurnal zones, section. 1. dining room; 2. sitting room; 3. smoking room; 4. portico; 5. dumb-waiter; 6. storeroom.

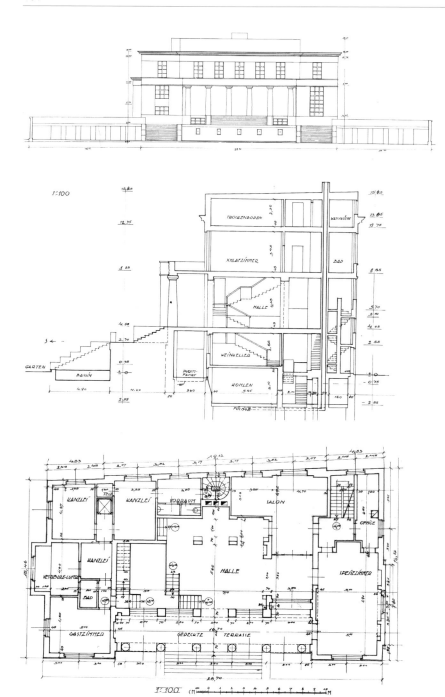

In this group of unrealized work, there is one other project of classical aspect: the villa for Dr. von Simon (Vienna, 1924; Fig. 89). The rigorously symmetrical ensemble evoked certain villas by Auguste Peret, whose work Loos admired (the Cassander House at Versailles, 1924; and Villa Nubar Bey at Garches, 1932). The Villa von Simon was composed of an elevated center (the core of the villa) and two smaller projecting wings reserved for special functions. A statue of Heracles stood in the middle of the villa's rectangular court, on axis with the recessed entrance. From the vestibule (equipped with a washbasin), one ascended to the dining room by two separate stairs. On the garden side, Loos again used a portico with symmetrically disposed stairs and columns.

As classical as they may seem, these four projects were, in fact, expressions of the dissolution of the language of classical architecture. Loos had no interest in making exact reproductions of his precedents, nor did he concern himself with the (lack of) archeological coherence of his compositions. What interested him was the effect these citations and fragments would have on the memory or architectural conscience of his contemporaries. He admitted to the breakdown of orders and styles and conceded that he used liberal combinations of isolated elements, but claimed that both were of little importance. The isolated elements transcended a hierarchy of parts to become lesser or greater than their models. Loos intended to renew the eighteenth-century tradition (that of Fischer von Erlach and the revolutionary French architects), a tradition extended into the nineteenth century in Germany by Karl Friedrich Schinkel.[28]

Loos also designed several vacation homes. As secondary residences inhabited only in the summer or in the winter, they had the same basic interior structure as the urban houses, but were more creatively, less strictly developed. Moreover, they were inserted in diverse contexts—at the sea or in the mountains—and these contexts were reflected in the work. Loos thought that the tradition of the region should guide the imagination of the architect: "Take notice of the forms of construction used by the peasant," he wrote in 1913. "In them is expressed an immemorial experience. But look for the reason for the forms. If technical

opposite page:

87a VILLA BRONNER: VIENNA, 1921.
     Main elevation.

87b,c VILLA BRONNER.
     Section and ground floor plan—*halle:* reception hall; *speisezimmer:* dining room; *kanzlei:* office; *vorraum:* antechamber; *gastzimmer:* guest room; *vestibule-luftraum:* winter garden; *bad:* bathroom; *schlafzimmer:* bedroom; *gedeckte terrasse:* covered terrace; *trockenboden:* drying room; *waschküche:* laundry; *weinkeller:* wine cellar; *kohlen:* coal cellar; *durchfahrt:* corridor; *garten:* garden; *füsche:* ash pit.

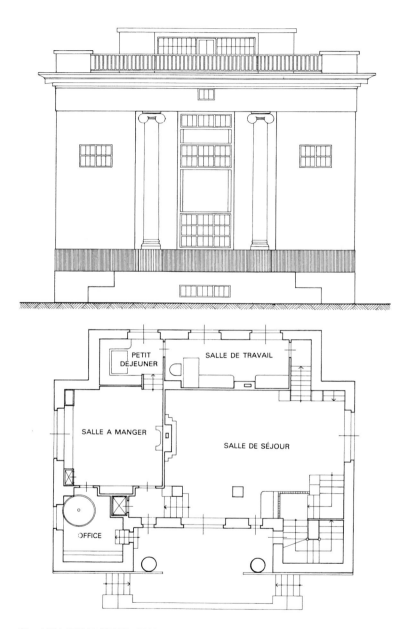

88 VILLA STROSS: VIENNA, 1922.
Garden elevation, plan of raised ground floor.

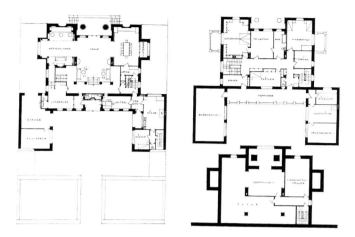

89a   VILLA VON SIMON: VIENNA, 1924.
      Plans: ground floor (left), basement and first floor (right).

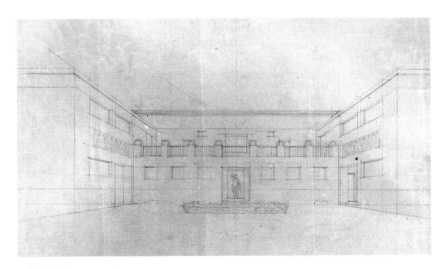

89b   VILLA VON SIMON.
      Perspective of main entrance.

90   VILLA VERDIER: LE LAVANDOU (NEAR TOULON), 1923.
Watercolor perspective.

progress allows you to ameliorate the process, it is necessary to adopt this amelioration
....Be true. Nature only supports the truth. She accepts iron-trussed bridges, but rejects
ornate gothic rib vaults of turrets and loopholes. Do not be afraid of being labeled unmod-
ern. You are permitted to change the accepted method of construction only if the innovation represents progress; if the opposite is true, preserve the tradition. Because the truth,
be it secular, is closer to our lives than the lies that march at our sides."[29]

The villa for the industrialist Paul Verdier was designed to be built in Lavandou, near
Toulon, close to the sea (1923, Figs. 90–91). It was a remarkable example of rational
Loosian architecture. Several volumes were symmetrically arranged in a composition as
complex on the inside as it was on the outside. The bearing walls were of ashlar, the floors,
concrete. There was no decoration, not even window casings: the openings were cut directly
into the walls. The symmetrical stair on the garden side was similar to the one used in the
Steiner House, but was convex, following the line of two half-cylinders on the facade. The
articulation was concentrated in the disposition of volumes and fenestration. On the inside,
the hierarchy of the living spaces was respected but was simplified. On the ground floor,
the high-ceilinged living room was surrounded by the dining room, the kitchen, and the
master and guest bedrooms. On the upper floor, a gallery which overlooked the living room
led to the servants' bedrooms. The garage and other related rooms were in the basement.

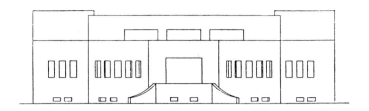

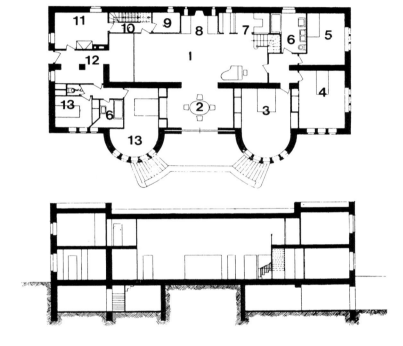

91   VILLA VERDIER.
Main elevation, ground floor plan, and longitudinal section. 1: living room; 2. dining room; 3. woman's bedroom; 4. man's bedroom; 5. daughter's room; 6. bathroom; 7. bar; 8. hearth; 9. pantry; 10. office; 11. kitchen; 12. closet; 13. guest room.

92   VILLA MOÏSSI: LIDO, VENICE, 1923.
      Model. The simplicity of the exterior contrasts the complexity of the interior volumes.

Loos's project for a vacation house for Alexander Moïssi, a celebrated actor of the time, was a rational transformation of Mediterranean vernacular architecture (Lido, Venice, 1923; Figs. 92–93). The composition was entirely subordinate to the conditions of the site: the quality and abundance of light and the proximity to the sea. A terrace with a pergola, accessible by an outside staircase, was level with and thus extended the living room; it was designed to be the center of the composition and of activity in the vacation home. Another terrace was designed for the roof, for private sunbathing by the Moïssis and their friends. The uncovered stair, the pure volumes, the flat roof, and the openings cut into the stark white stucco walls at once respected Mediterranean tradition and predated the smooth white boxes of Le Corbusier.

An L-shaped living zone grouped the living room, the hearth, the music room, and the dining room. This zone was extended out onto the terrace, sheltered by either leg of the L-shaped living area. The two bedrooms for the Moïssis, and the kitchen and a servant's room constituted two distinct zones that overlapped on two different levels beneath the living area. The guest rooms were situated under the kitchen and could exist autonomously from those of the Moïssis. Two service rooms and the guard's lodgings were located in the basement.

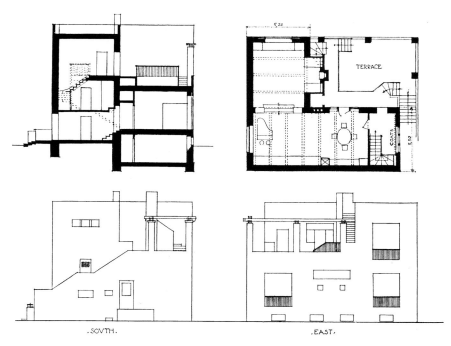

.SOVTH.   .EAST.

92   VILLA MOÏSSI.
Section, plan, and south and east elevations.

The most beautiful of Loos's vacation homes was designed for Paul Khuner. It was built
near Payerbach (1929–1930, Figs. 94–98), in the mountainous forests of Semmering in
Austria (it is now a hotel). A wood structure on a masonry base, the Khuner House was
built using local materials and traditional craftsmanship. Its brown framework rested on a
greenish stone, and the room partitions were of ordinary white wood. According to Heinrich
Kulka, who collaborated on the project, Loos had dreamed for thirty years of building such
a house.

The spatial fluidity of this structure was one of constantly shifting perspectives, axes,
and groupings. The principal room was double height. On the ground floor, it was surrounded by the dining room, the kitchen, Mr. Khuner's study, and two guest rooms. On the upper
floor, off the gallery that overlooked over the living room, were five bedrooms for the family,
two guest rooms, and two servant's rooms. The other service rooms were located in the
basement and the storehouse. The flexibility of the arrangement, based on the module of
the repetitive wood structure, the use of lively colors (the gallery's balustrades are red), the
intimacy of the bedrooms, the elegance of the living room with its hearth of green stone,

94   KHUNER HOUSE: KREUZBURG, PAYERBACH (AUSTRIA), 1929–1930.
      Side view. Photo: 1929.

95   KHUNER HOUSE.
      Main elevation. Photo: 1929.

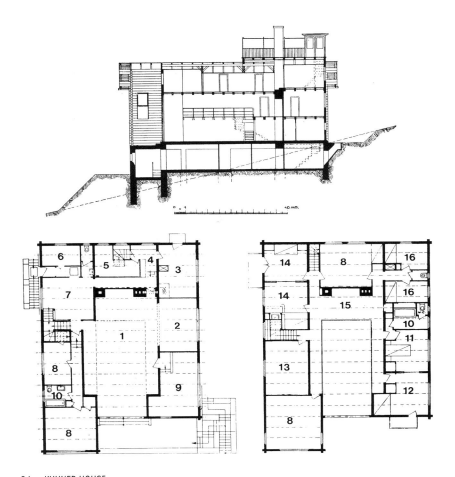

96   KHUNER HOUSE.
Section and ground floor and first floor plans. 1. sitting room; 2. dining room; 3. kitchen; 4; office; 5. pantry; 6. ski closet; 7. vestibule; 8. guest room; 9. man's office; 10. bathroom; 11. man's bedroom; 12. woman's bedroom; 13. son's bedroom; 14. daughters' bedroom; 15. gallery; 16. maid's room; 17. terrace.

and the spectacular view of the Schneeberg and Rax Mountains through the two-story window, all made the Khuner House a masterpiece.

The Khuner House was built using regional construction methods to seem at one with its site and the landscape. But nothing about the house was picturesque; though Loos knew to enrich his design by consulting and using the experience of masons and artisans, he still worked according to stringent aesthetic guidelines. He considered naive regionalism to be a ridiculous regression; a house built in nature ought to be and appear traditional, but it

97   KHUNER HOUSE.
Sitting room. Photo: 1930.

98   KHUNER HOUSE.
Sitting room. Photo: 1930. The balustrade is painted red.

should be built in the style of the architect who designed it, and it should conform to the times. The form and size of the fenestration, the vertical and horizontal sliding shutters, the deep overhang of the roof and its stepped support beams, and the roof terrace at the back were all elements that contradicted the style of the region. Though traditional, the Khuner House was still the product of modern rationalism.

CHAPTER FIVE
MIXED-USE BUILDINGS AND WORKERS' HOUSING

Evidence of Loos's interest in urban buildings dates from 1904, when he designed a branch
of a bank on the ground floor of an 1869 building. He proposed a total renovation of the
building's exterior: a new facade, stripped bare of all ornamentation (Fig. 99). This proposal predated the Looshaus in Vienna, a building he completed six years later (Fig. 106).
Loos wished to clearly differentiate the commercial area from the apartments on the four
upper floors. He designed the building to communicate to passersby the solid respectability
of the commercial establishment: "The bank must declare: here your money is secure and
well looked after by honest people."[1] At the same time, the upper floors introduced a radical and unprecedented simplicity; they consisted solely of rhythmically repetitive windows
piercing the smooth, white wall. The ceiling heights and windows of the apartments were of
equal size (except for two windows at the chamfered corner) to convey the equality of the
liberal bourgeois who would live in this curtain wall building. Social discrimination was not
projected on the facade; the exterior expressed no hierarchy whatsoever. This democratic
proposal was never built.

The Looshaus on Michaelerplatz in Vienna (1909–1911; Figs. 100–120) was a far more
influential project. The building contained apartments as well as the Goldman & Salatsch
clothing store. When the Looshaus was conceived, the plaza—Michaelerplatz—comprised
Saint Michael's Church, medieval with a classical facade (Fig. 105b, on the right), the
entry to the imperial palace's court of honor (built at the end of the nineteenth century from
a design by Fischer von Erlach, Fig. 103), the Herberstein mansion, and three bourgeois
houses, one of which would be replaced by the Looshaus. "It was a question of building a
new, modern, commercial building in the neighborhood of the imperial palace, and of
establishing a transition between the imperial palace—the palace of a nobleman—and the
most chic of our commercial streets, the Kohlmarkt."[2] Loos sought to create merely a mod-
est and functional building.

   The building owes its exceptional character to the strategic position that it occupied in
the historic context of Vienna. It symbolized the meeting of the medieval town and the
modern city, and the meeting of memory and of creation. Loos intended to create a building
well integrated with the urban fabric. As he explained in a letter of December 6, 1910,
published in the *Neue Freie Presse* under the title "The House that Faces the Hofburg," he
"conceived the house in such a manner that it would be integrated as much as possible into
the plaza. I derived my cornice lines from those of the church. If I chose this form of window, it was not to drive away air and light, but to multiply both, a legitimate claim of our

99   MULTI-STORY BANK AND RENOVATION OF APARTMENT BUILDING: VIENNA, 1904.
Photomontage: 1904.

times....I chose authentic marble because all imitation displeases me, and I reduced the decoration to a minimum because the Viennese bourgeoisie construct simply....I took great care to rigorously separate the offices from the apartments. I knew to resolve these problems in the manner of our former Viennese masters."[3]

The building, according to Loos, was simultaneously traditional and modern—through his attention to functional clarity—but sustained a great deal of opposition from the public, almost provoking an interruption of construction in 1910. Critics argued against the extreme simplicity of the upper portion—the housing—with its smooth, white stucco walls pierced with three-pane windows. However, the spare exterior was abandoned in the sumptuous interior of Goldman & Salatsch, consistent with the store's commercial reputation. Loos clad the walls and the columns of the main entrance and the mezzanine with cipolin marble from the Eubee. These materials were also used on the building's facade, to denote the difference between commercial and residential zones. Loos challenged the classical unity of the facade by combining two materially autonomous halves.

100 MICHAELERPLATZ BEFORE CONSTRUCTION OF LOOSHAUS.

101 MICHAELERPLATZ AFTER CONSTRUCTION OF LOOSHAUS.

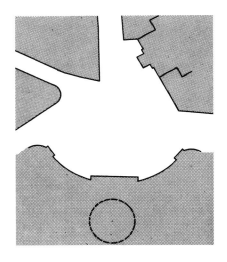

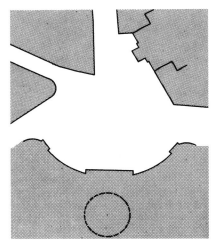

above:

102 MICHAELERPLATZ, 1898 TO 1909.
Drawings by H. Czech and W. Mistelbauer show
how Loos's intervention accentuated Michaelerplatz's
circularity.

left:

103 LOOSHAUS FROM ENTRANCE OF IMPERIAL PALACE.

104   MICHAELERPLATZ AFTER CONSTRUCTION OF LOOSHAUS.
The building at left was completed only ten years before Loos's.

The Looshaus was built with reinforced concrete, but its structure was not apparent on the facade, only on the interior court (Fig. 113). The plan of the building was adapted to the circulation around the plaza, which it consequently reconfigured (Fig. 102). Loos was diametrically opposed to the construction ethic that viewed the dissimulation of structural supports as an error, and the use of false supports as a crime; if they were, he was guilty of both. Loos felt that honesty in architecture did not necessarily mean exposing the structural skeleton, it was more reliant on cultural integrity (see Loos's definition of culture in chapter two, under 'Towards an Architecture without the Avant-Garde'). Karl Kraus, in defense of the Looshaus, declared that "[Loos] has built you a thought."[4]

The facade's Tuscan columns were purely symbolic. The heavy loads they seemed to carry were actually displaced onto side columns by a large beam that spanned the entire facade (Fig. 115). The smaller columns in the windows of the mezzanine (Figs. 105–106) were also structurally superfluous; the only strictly functional elements were the piers, whose form carried no stylistic reference. These columns of precious marble served only as fragmented quotations of traditional discourse.

Loos transgressed the rules of classical composition to suit his needs: the columns of the central entrance were lengthened by shafts, reversing the arrangement of the column and the pedestal; the steps were set out between rather than before the columns, and the too-thin lintel was very clearly an iron bar (Fig. 106).[5] Equally distant from classicism's addition of form to the basic functional nature of the column, and from Modernism's emphasis

105a RELATIONSHIP BETWEEN LOOSHAUS AND ITS CONTEXT.
Looshaus and Imperial Palace. Photographic analysis by Herman Czech.

105b RELATIONSHIP BETWEEN LOOSHAUS AND ITS CONTEXT.
Looshaus and Church of Saint Michael. Photographic analysis by Herman Czech.

106 LOOSHAUS: VIENNA, 1909–1911.
     Facade on Michaelerplatz. Photo: 1930.

solely on the column's more practical side, Loos used ornamental columns, devoid of structural justification. They contradicted the radical bareness of the upper portion of the building, and affirmed, in their uselessness, the presence of the illogical in an otherwise rational
architecture. Even the building's parti was neither traditional nor modern; it was determined by the cultural exigencies of the place and the moment. The Looshaus was neither a
sterile imitation of the Ancients nor the anticipation of modernist purism. Loos's work is
more understandable if it is not seen as a predecessor of the Modern Movement, but as a
reaction to the theories of his Viennese contemporaries on the material essence of style, the
thoughts of Gottfried Semper,[6] and the historic continuity of forms in the tradition of Aloïs
Riegl and the Vienna School.[7]

107 LOOSHAUS.
Facade detail. Photo: 1986.

108 LOOSHAUS.
Facade detail. Photo: 1986.

clockwise from top left:

109 LOOSHAUS.
Facade detail. Photo: 1986.

110 LOOSHAUS.
Detail of cornice separating commercial and residential zones. Photo: 1986.

111 LOOSHAUS.
Base of a portico column. A recent accident exposed the construction technique; column bases are thin metal shells, filled with cement (column capitols were made in the same manner). Photo: 1986.

112 LOOSHAUS.
View of cornice from Fig. 110, showing roof cornice above. Photo: 1986.

113 LOOSHAUS.
Interior court, showing structural clarity. Photo: c. 1975.

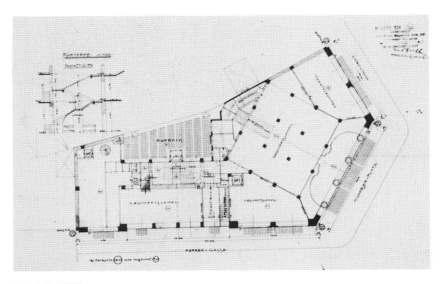

114 LOOSHAUS.
Ground floor plan. The square space was reserved for the Goldman & Salatsch store.

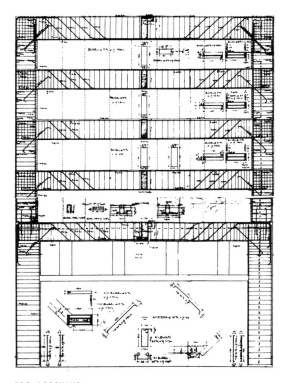

115 LOOSHAUS.
Structural plan of main elevation. Loos commissioned
"the firm of Pittel & Brausewetter, specialists in concrete
and reinforced concrete" to do the drawings. All weight rests
on the pile-ons; the Tuscan columns are not load-bearing.

116 LOOSHAUS.
Ground floor, Goldman & Salatsch. Photo: 1930.

117 LOOSHAUS.
Staircase, Goldman & Salatsch.

opposite page:

118 LOOSHAUS.
Entrance to apartments. Photo: c. 1930.

119 LOOSHAUS.
Entrance to apartments. The book-matched marble slabs suggest a human figure. Photo: 1986.

120 LOOSHAUS.
Entrance to apartments, detail of stair banister. One enters into a symmetrical space (see Fig. 118) after passing between two mirrors that create infinite reflections, then between the mysterious figures in the book-matched marble (Fig. 119), arriving at the stair, whose turn is marked by a lamppost. Photo: 1986.

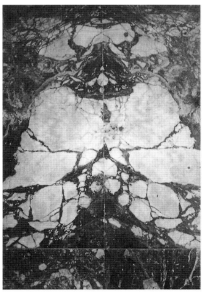

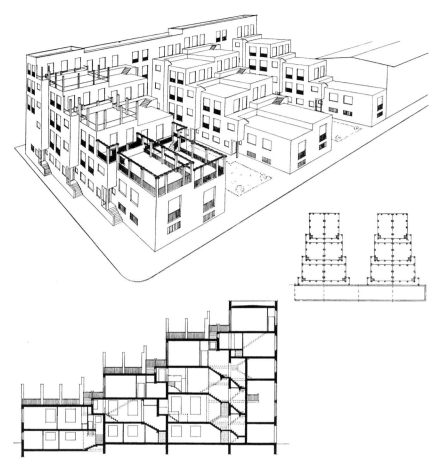

121 PROJECT FOR TWENTY "VILLAS": COTE D'AZUR, 1923.
Perspective, diagram of construction method, section.

Twelve years after completing the Looshaus, Loos proposed a community development of
vacation homes. This project for twenty "villas" on the Riviera, and a project he presented
at the Salon d'Automne of 1923, created a type somewhere between an apartment building
and a country house (Fig. 121). Free from the constraints of urban fabric, he grouped several apartments on a seaside resort site. The project's Mediterranean context conditioned all
aspects of the ensemble, and helped generate an ingenious solution to limited and expensive seaside property. The villas were arranged in such a way so that the roof of one served
as a terrace and garden of another. Each wing of villas was attached to a large bar function-

ing as a communal service core, and between each wing was a collective garden. The symmetrical grouping of the two wings of villas could be repeated indefinitely. The Mediterranean character was enhanced by numerous sets of steps between the different levels of the roofs and between the pergolas of the roof gardens. Despite the complexity of the interconnecting volumes—the Raumplan—the project was quite simple and bare.

As Chief Architect of the Housing Department of the Commune of Vienna, Loos became involved in the debate on garden cities. He made several proposals for workers' housing, proposals which revealed his views on social relations. He never proposed an ideal city on the scale of those of Le Corbusier or Frank Lloyd Wright; he was not interested in utopia. It was not that he was indifferent to modern urban problems, but he had a deep sense of a city's historicity, a fundamental factor in his projects. The workers' housing that he built in an impoverished area near Vienna and his 1926 lecture on modern workers' cities[8] were accurate representations of his ideas on the subject. Loos explained that a factory worker could neither obtain nor maintain a house with a garden. If he wanted to live off the produce in the garden, he could farm only after his eight-hour work day, in a garden of manageable size. The housing Loos designed featured gardens of 150 to 200 square meters (1615 to 2150 square feet), enclosed between walls to limit the effects of wind and sun, and oriented north-south to benefit from the sun at its zenith.[9] Even where the streets did not follow a rigorous east-west axis, the orientation of the gardens had to be maintained and the houses were aligned in a serrated formation. Between each house and garden was a small courtyard with a tool shed and a rabbit hutch (Fig. 122). The houses were comprised of two levels corresponding to diurnal and nocturnal activities. On the ground floor was a dining room and kitchen—the center of domestic life—as large as possible a pantry, an outhouse, and an entrance from the street. The floor above held three bedrooms for the parents, the girls, and the boys. This arrangement remained relatively flexible, as the intermediate partitions were often installed at a later date. The bedrooms were small and low to discourage lounging: "In the bedroom, I undress, I go to bed, I sleep, I get up, and I get dressed. That is what it is for and one should not enter during the day. Living and sleeping should be separated."[10]

The houses were attached, built by a construction method to reduce the cost and to increase the number of units without compromising the durability and quality of the housing. With economy in mind, in 1921 Loos patented a system of construction "with a wall": a simple system of standard wood beams between lateral walls.[11] In proposing this unorthodox method—one foreign to official norms—Loos introduced and campaigned for the potential of artisan tradition in a time of serial production. However, the elementary technique that he proposed was far from the sophisticated methods of modular construction that were developing at the time. It was the division of space that was more radical: the interior

122 WORKERS' HOUSING: 1921.

was divided by armoires, drapes, and movable panels. But Loos's ideas on daily life in workers' cities were considered anachronistic and simplistic, and they were contrary to those being pursued by the city of Vienna, which envisaged large buildings laid out around common courtyards (*Hofe*). When the situation became a conflict, Loos decided to renounce his first and last official job, but he continued to plan and design workers' housing for the city and for private developers.

Loos's interest in collective habitation revealed his hopes for using architecture to correct what he saw as society's ills. The Loos of *Siedlungen* (workers' housing) was antithetical to the Loos of the *better neighborhoods*. His individual residences were imbued with his insistence on the intimacy and durability of the home. While in the case of a bourgeois apartment building, his first concern was contextual continuity, he also aimed at the best possible layout of rooms within the predetermined shape. His interiors catered to the habits

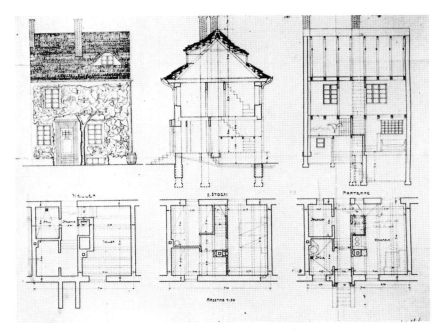

123 HIRSCHTETTEN WORKERS' HOUSING: VIENNA, 1921.
Each house measured seven meters (twenty-three feet) wide.

124 WORKERS' HOUSING: 1921.
Street elevation of a scheme presented at a conference in London, 1922.

of his clients, as evidenced by his interior renovations (see chapter 3). Conversely, the workers' housing, situated far from the historic city center, excluded all personalization. Attention was given to the simple layout of practical plans and to the creation of a type to which the lives of all the inhabitants were required to conform. Loos's workers' housing was notable for its emphasis on the impermanence of its construction, its habit-shaping spatial configuration, and its conditioning of daily activities. With these residences, the task of the architect was focused on regularizing the plans and keeping costs down.

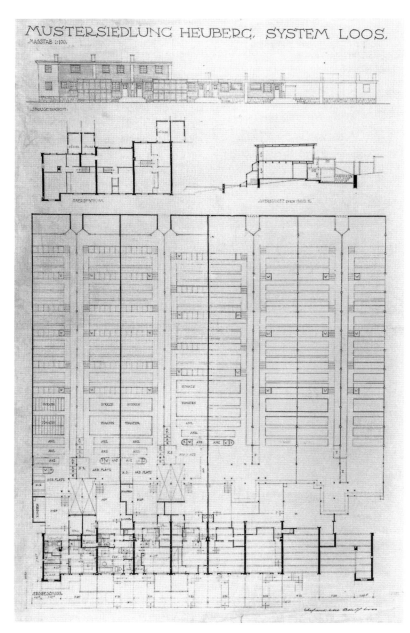

125 HEUBERG WORKERS' HOUSING: VIENNA, 1921.
  Street elevation, sections, and plans of the houses and their gardens.

126 AUSTRIAN *WERKBUND* WORKERS' HOUSING: VIENNA, 1932.
     South elevation of house by Adolf Loos.

At the beginning of the 1920s, Loos collaborated on the master plans for several workers'
cities for Vienna (among them, the garden cities of Friedensstadt, Heuberg, and Laarberg).
Concurrently, he was working on prototypical housing for these cities, developing a living
scheme based on the family unit. The three types of workers' housing found in Loos's work
are actually variations on one basic type: a two-story house with a garden. The first and
most traditional variation was used in Lainz and in Hirschstetten (1921); four masonry
walls delineated each family's space, and a single pitched roof covered a long bar of several houses (Fig. 123). A second variation, presented at a 1922 conference in London, featured more complex spatial configurations and flat roofs (Fig. 124). Loos was looking to
both make an architectural statement and to establish a certain flexibility on the facade.
The last variation, used for the housing at Heuberg (1921; Fig. 125), was a pared-down,
rational revision of the first type. Loos retained the idea of the housing forming a bar, but
he employed a flat roof and used wood frame construction—"with a wall"—for quickly and
inexpensively built housing. Unfortunately, although the construction was time- and cost-
effective, it was not particularly durable.

At the beginning of the 1930s, Loos was invited to participate in the construction of an
international workers' city in Vienna, organized by the Austrian *Werkbund*. Since the

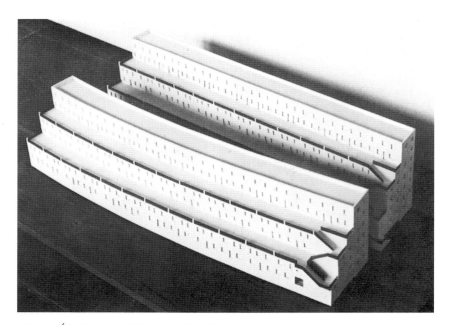

127 UNITÉ D'HABITATION WITH GRADED TERRACES: VIENNA, 1923.
Model.

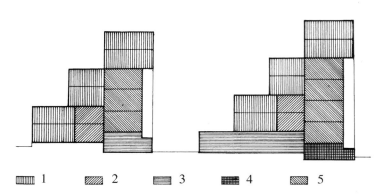

128 UNITÉ D'HABITATION WITH GRADED TERRACES.
Volumetric diagrams by B. Rukschcio and R. Schachel. 1. two-story apartments; 2. circulation; 3. workshops;
4. studios; 5. small one-story apartments.

founding of the *Werkbund*, Loos had often criticized its theoretical and cultural program. Yet he accepted their invitation, and constructed a group of four houses (Fig. 126), similar to his workers' housing of the 1920s but slightly "modernized" in appearance. He also introduced a mezzanine between the two floors to extend the living room. These model homes, intact and in excellent condition, represent the successful culmination of Loos's ideas on and experiments with serial construction.

In 1923, Loos proposed a housing complex for the city of Vienna which was never built (Fig. 127). This somber and rational residential complex of terraced setbacks, situated on a curved street, made no stylistic concession to history. Loos saw no reason for architecture for the working classes to cater to either nostalgia or a "proletarian style," as its simplicity, he felt, was incontestable. Loos's scheme consisted of small apartments, nearly half of which were two stories (Fig. 128). This layout, developed on the scale of a housing complex, represented a remarkable novelty in Europe at that time. "People believed," explained Loos, "that their living rooms should not adjoin their bedrooms; they like to access the latter by a stair. They imagine then that they have their own house, which gives them a better opinion of themselves."[12] Regardless, the most salient elements of Loos's project were the large communal terraces which were meant to function as raised streets and meeting places: "Each person possesses his own entrance with his own outdoor space where he can sit at the end of the day and take in some fresh air. It is possible for children to play on the terrace without worrying about being hit by a car....My tranquil and protected terraces give the children the possibility of spending the whole day out of doors, near their apartment and under the neighbors' surveillance."[13] The ingenuity of this unrealized work lay in its common sense approach and its attention to the lives and requirements of its inhabitants, not on formal research or political convictions.

CHAPTER SIX
MONUMENTAL BUILDINGS AND LARGE PROJECTS

For Loos, urban architecture could not exist without a connection to its context. He felt that civic buildings and the monuments of a city should be considerate to urban and cultural history. Through their buildings, architects can both communicate concepts and influence lives, and must recognize that the atmosphere particular to a city lies in the sediment of memory, history, and urbanism.

Loos differentiated between residences (individual and collective) and singular elements (public buildings and symbolic places). He believed that the city consisted of a grid of singular elements whose interstices were filled by anonymous residential areas. This was the commonly held conception of urban form prior to the birth of the Modern Movement, and for Loos, it demanded that one respect the coherence of the existing fabric. His theories on urbanism, based on the collective comprehension of morphological continuity, are an important source for today's architects, such as Aldo Rossi.[1]

Unfortunately, Loos never published a comprehensive text on his ideas about urbanism. What we know of his pursuits in this realm have been culled from certain idealistic or utopian sketches—probably didactic exercises—and from references in his other writings. Yet his large urban projects, always meticulously documented and fully developed, even if never realized, eloquently expressed his ideas about the city: the commemorative monument to the Emperor Franz-Josef, the administrative tower for *The Chicago Tribune*, and the renovation of Modenapark, to name a few.

Loos's works were greatly inspired by the urban theoretician Camillo Sitte.[2] According to Burkhardt Rukschcio,[3] several of Sitte's fundamental principles were adopted by Loos: maximum preservation of the old city, comprehension of the needs and aspirations of the inhabitants, and a rapport of reciprocity and exchange in the handling of volumes and spaces. For Sitte as for Loos, the lessons of history intervene decisively in a city's development.

Additionally, Loos relied on a system of traditional thinking in founding the organization of monumental space on the classical ideas of symmetry, proportion, and perspective. But his return to tradition does not translate into a simple imitation of historic characteristics, it is instead an understanding of and respect for the past, leading to a formulation of an architecture for the present. Loos admired classical forms outside their original context, those that could be appropriated from the great modern cultures. He believed that elements of classical architecture foreign to Vienna could create an architecture that was altogether Viennese, just as Oriental spices, used judiciously, allowed and enlivened an authentic Austrian cuisine.[4]

With the hybridization, distillation, and denigration of the orders, the scales, the hierarchies, and of the classical language in general at the beginning of the twentieth century, Loos conceived of monumental architecture as the conceptualized reprise of the tradition that had flowered in Germanic countries in the first two thirds of the nineteenth century (Friedrich Gilly, Karl Friedrich Schinkel, Leo von Klenze). All the constituent elements of a building—windows, stairs, proportions, symmetry—could grow rich with symbolic weight and nourish the city with their complexity and historicity.

The distinction in this chapter, between monumental projects and projects of a more utilitarian order, is based upon Loos's distinction between art and architecture—the monument and the tomb being, in his eyes, the only buildings appropriate to the first category.[5]

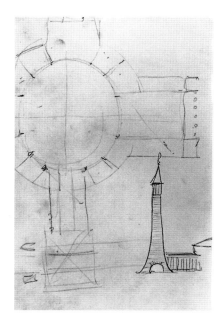

129 SAINT ELIZABETH CHURCH, VIENNA, 1898.
Three sketches.

Monuments and Monumental Buildings

On the occasion of an 1898 competition for the construction of Saint Elizabeth Church in Vienna commemorating the jubilee of the Emperor, Adolf Loos designed a project of which, unfortunately, only three sketches remain (Fig. 129). The project illuminated Loos's reflections on monumental urban architecture. His proposal consisted of a church of elliptical plan and a tall tower of about fifty meters (165 feet), terminating a straight avenue that connected the center of Vienna and the Danube quay to Mexicoplatz. The commemorative monument was not treated as an isolated entity, as it had to engage the collective conscience of the city's inhabitants as well as close one of the city's perspectives. It was also a reflection or twin of the tower of the Cathedral of Saint Etienne, the principal religious monument of old Vienna, which was situated along the same avenue.

The other startling aspect of this first project was the predominance of classical models, as much in the composition of the plan as in the details of the facade. The reference to the Pantheon (second century A.D.) was clear, especially on the interior—even though Loos

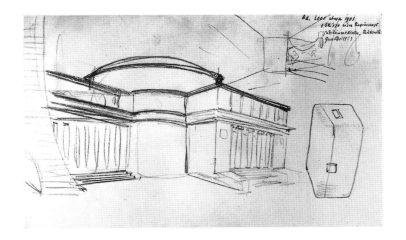

130 SKETCHES FOR A THEATER, c. 1900.

used an ellipse rather than a perfect circle, and he multiplied the portico columns of the celebrated Roman monument by four. The tower was a strange combination of the mausoleum of Halicarnasse (placed at the summit, with a figure dressed as an emperor) and the profile of the Eiffel Tower. Loos had sought to create unity from disparate sources. Influenced by American neoclassicism, which he discovered on his apprenticeship voyage, he leaned more on Roman monumental tradition than on Greek art.

The Romans attached great importance to the layout and the division of their buildings; they looked for harmony in plan and proportion. Moreover, they drew from all the available forms of the era and rearticulated the known to produce the new; one can say the same of Loos. He praised the genius of the Romans in pointing out (as a positive trait) their incapacity to invent "a new column order, or a new ornament," although they "administered the globe."[6]

Loos also strove to combine the forms and signs of the past to express the spirit of his own time. He hoped for the widespread acceptance of his aesthetic, and if he borrowed from a succession of classicisms—from Roman to nineteenth-century, from Palladio to Schinkel—he did so in search of forms that would be most evocative to the collective memory (Fig. 130). There was no attention to archeological loyalty: he took ancient forms and detached them from their original context by giving them soft and uncertain contours and an aura that muddled their identity. Repeated use over time had made these elements into references with which modern man could identify. They communicated a sense of history to a large number of people, and helped develop a more expressive architecture.[7]

These aims were first achieved in Loos's project for a new War Ministry (Figs. 131–132). The Ministry's previous building was a five-story classical composition in the am Hofplatz, built in the eighteenth century by Franz Hillebrand. In 1891, it was completed and its equestrian statue of the famous Marshall Radetzky was unveiled. The transfer of the Ministry to the Ring was decided in 1907, and the competition was announced. Only the statue was to be preserved, which was one of the requirements for all proposals.

Hillebrand's building was typical of the architecture of the end of the eighteenth century; Loos admired it for its rationalism and for its relationship to the classical tradition. When he was asked during an interview what was, according to him, the most beautiful of the buildings condemned to disappear, he responded without hesitation: "The War Ministry on the Hof. Look at it carefully, Viennese, because soon it will no longer be. Everyone knows that it will be demolished soon, but no voice has been raised to prevent this crime. Therefore, while there is still time, look at the Hof carefully to preserve it in your heart. This building gives a balance to the whole square. Without it, the Hofplatz will cease to exist."[8] In this sense, Loos's participation in the competition was an homage to the condemned building. But his project, entered under the pseudonym *Homo*, was judged not to conform to the rules and was eliminated.

For Loos, the city consisted of streets and plazas determined by the shape of and gaps between the urban fabric. Therefore, he did not see the Ministry as an autonomous structure; its form had to subordinate itself to its immediate environment, thus he derived the plan to comply with the irregular contours of the site (Fig. 132). Yet at the same time, as much as possible, he tried to create the symmetries he felt were appropriate to monumental architecture. It was for this reason that the main facade on the Ring was dominated by four

131a,b   WAR MINISTRY, VIENNA, 1907: MAIN FACADE.
The walls were to be yellow terracotta; the columns, black granite.

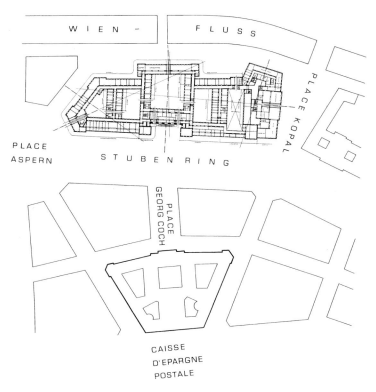

132 WAR MINISTRY.
Building plan in context, showing deference to local geometries.

projecting towers and by a large, recessed central court featuring the statue of Radetzky and the principle entrance to the Ministry (Fig. 131a). However, to situate the building on the axis formed by Georg Coch platz and by Otto Wagner's 1903 savings bank, Loos had to shift the recess to the left and, consequently, the axis of symmetry of the building was affected as well (Fig. 132). The two wings of the facade were no longer equal, but the imposing presence of the recessed court helped to neutralize this asymmetry. Loos had respected the perspectives and the form of the city at the expense of perfect autonomy for his building. In the same way, the facades giving onto the river, the side street, and onto Aspern and Kopal platzes were characterized by regularity and symmetry. All deformations were absorbed by the interior of the building. Except for the primary axis, the various axes of symmetry that determined the facades had no correspondence to the interior layout. Loos's entry to the War Ministry competition had been designed from the outside in. The

133 DEPARTMENT STORE, ALEXANDRIA, EGYPT, 1910.
     Watercolor perspective by R. Wels, a student of Loos.

complex maneuvers necessary to create an impressive and expressive monument had to be resolved on the interior, in a realm whose practical modes of organization did not at all concern the observer of urban theater.[9]

According to the notes that accompanied Loos's project, the facade on the Ring was to be quite bare, in contrast to the more ornate, monumental center. Loos was convinced that "his design was not there to captivate the spectator (*Beschauer*)."[10] Rather than to captivate, it was to communicate, without the aid of inscriptions and emblems, that it was a ministry. "But the artist, the *architect*," Loos wrote in 1898, "first senses the effect that he intends to realize and sees the room he wants to create in his mind's eye. He senses the effect that he wishes to exert upon the spectator: fear and horror if it is a dungeon, reverence if a church, respect for the power of the state if a government palace, piety if a tomb, homeyness if a residence, gaiety if a tavern. These effects are produced by both the material and the form of the space."[11] From the beginning of his career, one sees that Loos clearly defined his idea of an *architecture parlante*. In his War Ministry, respect for political power and the impression of solidity and security are obtained through the regularity of the visible parts and by the color of the materials. The walls of cut yellow stone and the black polished granite twin columns of the recessed entrance (Fig. 131b) represent the official colors of the monarchy.

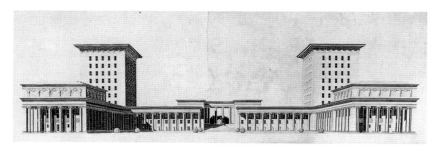

134 COMMEMORATIVE MONUMENT TO THE GLORY OF EMPEROR FRANZ-JOSEF AND CELEBRATED AUSTRIANS,
VIENNA, 1917.
Perspective.

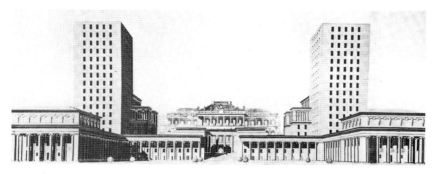

135 COMMEMORATIVE MONUMENT.
Variation on scheme: montage by L. Münz showing Koburg palace in background, c. 1950.

The predominance of the visible, articulate surfaces of the facades over the internal organization was also a determining factor in Loos's proposal for a department store in Alexandria, Egypt (1910). This project was one of Loos's favorites: a watercolor perspective, by his student R. Wels, hung in his living room (Fig. 133). The strange, rectangular, and monolithic building, a combination of the utilitarian and the sacred, brings to light the ambiguity of an urban architecture whose modern capabilities and requirements contrasted with Hellenistic and Oriental symbolism. The large ionic columns, the cornices, and the four upper floors (with Doric peristyles) in the shape of a ziggurat formed a composition of elements isolated from their original semantic codes, but adapted and recomposed in an original syntax. The Alexandria department store appeared as a fragment of spectacular scenography expressing the astonishing atmosphere of a metropolis both cosmopolitan and steeped in ancient Ptolemaic memory.

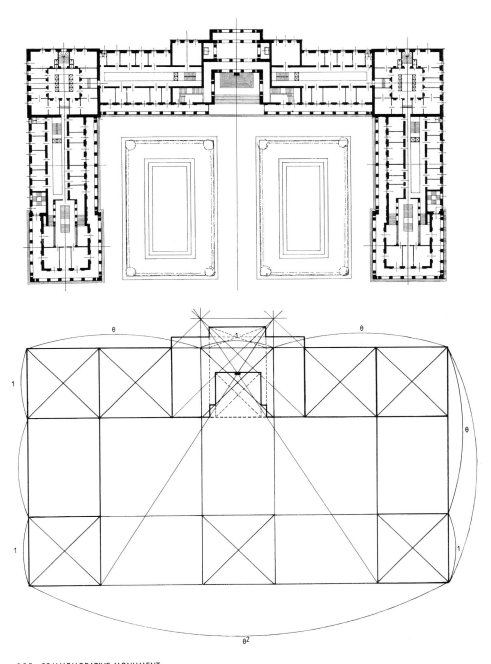

135 COMMEMORATIVE MONUMENT.
Plan and diagram.

137 COMMEMORATIVE MONUMENT.
    Sketch, with profile of Vienna Cathedral (at right).

Loos considered reciprocity to be the point of departure for all urban interventions. In his proposals for the Saint Elizabeth Church, the War Ministry, and the Alexandria department store, he had to work within the confines of a dense and constraining urban fabric. Yet his project for a monument dedicated to the Emperor Franz-Josef and celebrated Austrians, planned for a large esplanade on the grounds of the Horticultural Association (Vienna, 1917, Figs. 134–137), escaped these constraints. Because of the enormity of its scale, it was with the entire city that the monument had to establish a relationship. Its size and relative isolation allowed Loos far more freedom than usual, and his project became an acute criticism of the discontinuity of the Ring,[12] guaranteeing that it would remain on paper. The project is thus seen as an exercise in style or, a bit more cynically, a lesson in architecture.

The Horticultural Association occupied a garden on the Ring near Stadtpark, on which stood an exhibition pavilion built in the 1860s. Once used as a tennis and social club, the pavilion later became a cabaret popular with officers avidly seeking amusement, as described by Karl Kraus in the introduction to his Austrian tragedy, *The Last Days of Humanity*. But the site was primarily an open space on the edge of the city, from which one could enjoy unobstructed views of the Koburg Palace (1864), an elaborate neoclassical building. Loos's proposal was to fill the space with a commemorative complex, monumental yet welcoming, that would function simultaneously as an iconographic reference point for the city and as an area for gatherings and popular diversions for its inhabitants.

This project was in no way related to the modernist discourse of its time; it seemed more derrière than avant-garde. Loos had proposed a rectangular plaza surrounded by a U-shaped, classical building. The rigorously symmetrical composition focused on the rear of the plaza, on a stair enclosed by a portico distantly reminiscent of the ancient Propylaea.[13] At the top of the steps was a statue of the emperor on his throne. The plaza was ringed by an ionic colonnade, a gallery dedicated to celebrated Austrians. The galleries opened into side pavilions, museums commemorating the lives of these illustrious citizens. Two large towers reinforced the symmetry and the solemnity of the project. These towers were purely functional and were to be used by public organizations. The imposing complex had the feeling of a *metafisica* painting, with its hovering memory of so many illustrious dead.

The plan obeyed certain regulating principles. It seems to have been drawn over a perfect geometric grid whose proportions were regulated by irrational series of the square root of two and theta equalling one plus the square root of two (Fig. 136). All of its parts—plaza, colonnade, galleries, main building, and towers—were inextricably linked to each other and to the whole. Moreover, Loos's proposal was visually linked to the Koburg Palace by a common axis of symmetry. The montage by Ludwig Muntz (Fig. 135) shows how Loos intended to combine the two architectures to attain a dimension of the sublime.[14] Although one thinks—especially for the base—of Schinkel or Klenze, Loos's monument to Franz-Josef is not neoclassical pastiche. By opposing the main building and the two towers (and by radicalizing this opposition in another variation on the same project, Fig. 135), Loos did not simply mix styles: he separated functions, a more modern idea. The lower portion, being a commemorative monument, was beaux-arts; the towers, being utilitarian, were stripped clean of ornament. The bare purity of the functional zone opposed the classicism of the project's more monumental aspects.

Loos's main objective was to create a place dedicated to the memory of all those who had played a decisive role in the destiny of the country. Yet such a space was useless if it remained deserted; it had to attract and accommodate crowds. Such was the *raison d'être* for the rectangular plaza opening onto the Stadtpark; one could walk along the esplanade and participate in any ceremony or event held at the monument. The monument was to become a point of assembly (like the Palace of Chaillot, twenty years later), one which would benefit from large crowds. The two high towers (about 140 meters, or 460 feet) would rise above the city and would join the bell tower of Saint Etienne as principle reference points on the Viennese skyline. Loos, in his sketches, related the form and the height of his towers to the highest bell tower in the city, demonstrating his preoccupation with urban scale (Fig. 137).

138 PALACE OF LEISURE, MODENAPARK, VIENNA, 1922.
View of rectangular plaza from terrace of gaming room.

As his renderings testify—more precise than his sketches, by definition and by their link to realized projects—Loos worked passionately on this project, although it too was never built. Regardless, he believed in the didactic and critical potential of his ideas. It was in this same polemical spirit that he conceived the development of a large cultural forum in the northern part of Modenapark in Vienna (Figs. 138–139), even if it is the project's architectural qualities more than Loos's protestations against the politics of the city that interest us. At the beginning of the 1920s, the future of the park was examined and new construction was envisioned (which was actually realized in the 1950s). As a counterproposal to the idea of a cultural forum, Loos designed a Palace of Leisure. His proposed building was a composition of numerous recreational units: cafe, restaurant, hotel, skating rink, dance floor, gaming room, billiards room, and lecture hall. One entered through a large octagonal courtyard. The courtyard was flanked by two towers, tall enough to attract the citizens of Vienna (Fig. 139). Two enclosed, colonnaded, rectangular plazas formed a large assembly and promenade space in the tradition of the Roman *fora*. Loos aspired to create, in the heart of a modern city, a place that would mix culture and leisure, social relations and popular pleasures.

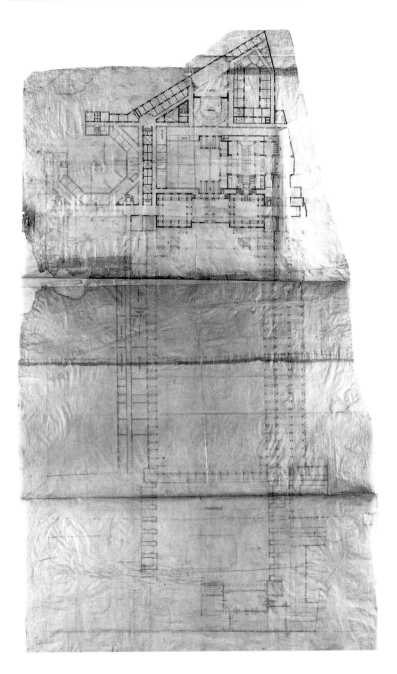

138 MODENAPARK.
     General plan.

140a SKETCHES FOR *CHICAGO TRIBUNE*
COMPETITION, 1922.

The surrounding walls of Loos's Palace of Leisure played a dual role. Facing the palace, they testified to Loos's love of geometry, symmetry, and rational classicism. Facing the city, they respected the continuity of the town and adapted to the urban fabric. To preserve the geometric purity of the interior, the wall's exterior was deformed and broken, completely subordinate to both Loos's design and the site's irregular context. Despite the complexity of the wall, it allowed the town to conserve its historic form and the buildings their geometric rigor, despite Loos's extensive tailoring (Fig. 139). In this approach, at once traditional and modern,[15] one can measure the distance that separated Loos from the *tabula rasa* urbanists of the Modern Movement.

The last and most celebrated of Loos's monumental projects was his competition entry for *The Chicago Tribune* tower. Celebrated as much as criticized, Loos's design continues to receive mixed reviews. In 1922, on the occasion of its seventy-fifth birthday, *The Chicago Tribune*, one of the biggest American newspapers of its time, launched a competition for a new administrative headquarters. The challenge was "to build the most beautiful office building in the world, and the most distinguished." The competition jurors received an overwhelming response; 260 projects were sent from 32 countries. Loos was very enthusiastic over his entry (sent from Nice as a French submission) but received neither an award nor even a mention (Figs. 140a–d).

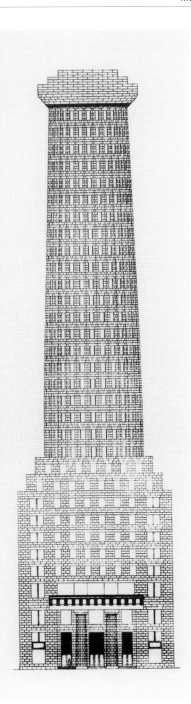

140b *CHICAGO TRIBUNE* COMPETITION ENTRY.
Elevation of tower.

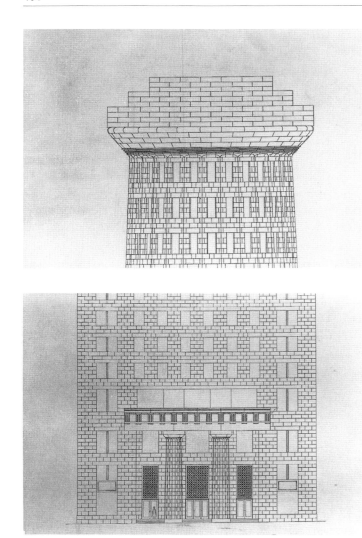

140c,d *CHICAGO TRIBUNE* COMPETITION ENTRY.
Details of facade.

Loos had written his intentions in a short brochure that accompanied his plans. He explained his desire to create a building that, seen only once, it would impress itself indelibly on the individual memory as the symbol of Chicago, in the way that St. Peter's incarnates Rome, and the leaning tower, Pisa. He recognized that it would be futile to hope to attain this objective when competing with skyscrapers of exceptional originality, already inscribed in history, or to reproduce a typical American building on which none would remark. Conversely, to adopt radical new forms that denied tradition—as did the proposals by several German, Austrian, and French architects—was to go against the mandate of the competition committee. Styles in non-traditional architecture were changing as frequently as women's hats, and the financial partners of the *Tribune* would not want to have made the mistake of choosing an avant-garde approach, only to discover that their once fashionable building had become dated the following year.

Loos, in presenting his column building, argued for the use of historical precedent: "The model of the column liberated from its function, of the gigantic column, is given to us by tradition: the column of Trajan was the model for the column of Napoleon in the Place Vendôme."[16] The triumphal column of the Roman emperor had symbolized the growth and power of the Roman empire and Loos's proposal could express the same for the *Tribune*. Additionally, the single column was an object that, since the Renaissance, had continually intrigued architects. Superb columns were represented in all architectural treatises that had been inspired by Vitruvius's *Ten Books*. Parted from practical functions and freed from load-bearing purposes, the column could affirm and assert its formal purity.

Loos's column was Doric, of black polished granite. It stood on an eleven-story base of brick and terracotta, with the exception of the black granite cornices and columns of the portico that marked the entrance. The color and style of the base were attempts at urban continuity, whereas the column was intended to pierce the Chicago skyline: "The smooth polished walls and the fluting of the Doric column must conquer the spectator," claimed Loos, who who often strove for the spectacular; "they will stun and cause a sensation in our blasé modern era."[17] Traditionally, triumphant columns are crowned by a figure, either sitting (as at the Greek theater of Dionysus in Athens), or standing (as at the Roman temple of Jupiter at Agrigente). Loos's, however, culminated in a stylized abacus. His column was not meant to be the bearer of a glorious statue of a deity or an allegory; it was a metaphor for the newspaper itself, which had become a "pillar" of society. A strong concept, a symbolic value, a monumental dimension—such was the essence of urban architecture for Loos.

Since its proposal in 1922, the opinion of historians and architects on this colossal Doric column has continued to vary; it has been considered as much an insignificant, absurd, and deceptive project, undignified to mention, as much as it has been seen as a fundamental and revolutionary project of incontestable and inexhaustible richness. For half a century, only the projects which attracted the favor of modernist criticism were mentioned and analyzed

141a ADOLF LOOS. *CHICAGO TRIBUNE* COMPETITION ENTRY.

141b PAUL GERHARD. *CHICAGO TRIBUNE* COMPETITION ENTRY.

—those of Gropius, Meyer, the Taut brothers, Ludwig Hilberseimer, the elder Saarinen, and a few others.[18] Then, in turn, the postmodernists thought that in Loos's column they had discovered an anti-modernist provocation, and the earliest example of postmodernism itself. Regardless, Loos's column was not really all that shocking or extraordinary, and at the time, it was thought banal. First prize in the competition was awarded to a gothic tower, while an immense Assyrian column and a Hellenistic temple on a high plinth were given honorable mentions. Loos himself stated in a notice that, among American skyscrapers in general, those whose architecture was the most satisfactory—the Metropolitan Building (N. Le Brun & Sons, New York, 1909) and the Woolworth Building (Cass Gilbert, New York, 1911–1913)—were based on the mausoleum at Halicarnassus and on the gothic tower. In the competition, three other projects had been designed in the same spirit as Loos's, and presented columns from various periods of antiquity, on rectangular bases: Matthew Freeman, Doric (Fig. 141c); Erich Patelsku, Corinthian (Fig. 141d); and P. Gerhard,

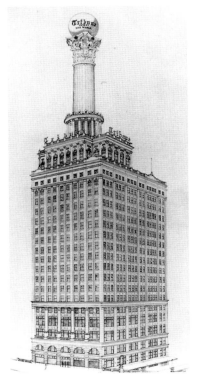

141c M. FREEMAN. *CHICAGO TRIBUNE* COMPETITION ENTRY.

141d ERICH PATELSKU. *CHICAGO TRIBUNE* COMPETITION ENTRY.

Egyptian (Fig. 141b).[19] The Egyptian column was distinguished from Loos's column only by a difference in style. As it was merely one of several column proposals, one can see that Loos's was not terribly surprising or revolutionary, although as a group, the proposals did challenge the "modern" project that Gropius and Meyer had sent from the Weimar Bauhaus.

Utilitarian Buildings

Loos designed several projects of a utilitarian nature, all of which are of incontestable importance because they epitomize certain essential dimensions of his architecture. The utilitarian buildings show Loos's skill at and ease with juxtaposing classical composition with purist elevations. These buildings, never realized, have certain traits in common: compact and massive aspect, symmetry of plan and facade, geometric order of forms, large smooth walls pierced by regularly divided windows, flat roofs, and the absence of ornament. Their layout is generally rectangular or U-shaped, and the axis of symmetry of the principle facade tends to carry through to the plan as well. The continuity of urban form is systematically respected; deformations imposed by the fabric of the city are absorbed in plan without affecting the regularity of the facades.

The majority of Loos's utilitarian projects are hotels. Loos, as mentioned, moved from one city to another and travelled often; he was particularly interested in temporary housing. The functional organization, the social and cultural character, and the atmosphere of these buildings were in some way tied to his personal life. In 1906 he participated in a private competition for a hotel on Friedrichstrasse in Vienna (Fig. 142). It was to be a luxurious establishment of 260 rooms and 200 suites, with every modern amenity including central heating, an underground garage, and elevators. Loos's proposal was well integrated in its context, occupying an entire trapezoidal site on the Karlplatz (Fig. 142b). Its simple exterior configuration reflected the order of the city. The angled but symmetrical principle facade was organized around a projecting volume—the portico and lobby—and this axis of symmetry penetrated to the central court of the building and determined the distribution of the common rooms. According to Loos, the lobby had been conceived and designed in the American manner, as a continuation of the street. It was a covered forum allowing protected passage to the outdoor seating terraces of the cafe and tea salon. A winter garden and a large elliptical restaurant were situated on either side of the lobby. The end wall of the lobby was mirrored, to optically double the already enormous space. This initial public zone was faultlessly composed, perpendicular to the angle of the main facade. Any necessary deformations from the reconciliation of this progression with the rest of the plan were accommodated by the hidden irregular service spaces. A second, cruciform dining room was located in the right angle of the back facade. It was a perfectly formed entity, with a single, peripheral connection to the main dining room. In these spaces and as a whole, Loos's proposal was classified by sumptuous architecture subordinate to rigorous order, as much on the interior as on the exterior.

142a HOTEL, FRIEDRICHSTRASSE, VIENNA, C. 1906.
   Main facade.

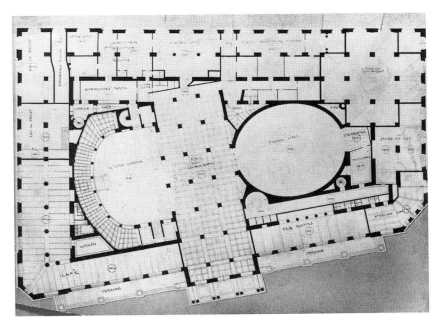

142b HOTEL, FRIEDRICHSTRASSE.
   Ground floor plan.

143a HOTEL, CHAMPS-ÉLYSÉES, PARIS, 1924.
Perspective.

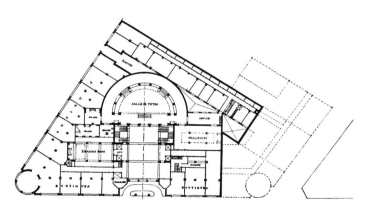

143b HOTEL, CHAMPS-ÉLYSÉES.
Ground floor plan.

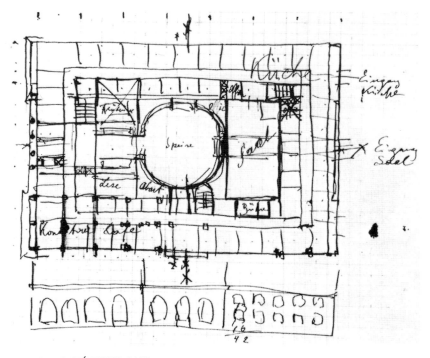

144   HOTEL CLARTÉ, ZAGREB, 1921.
Sketch of ground floor plan on graph paper.

Loos's next large hotel project was eighteen years later, for a luxury hotel on the Champs-Élysées, between rue La Boétie and rue du Colisée (Fig. 143). One finds the same desire for a compositional regularity on the facade that continues in the plan (despite the complicated shape of the site), as in the hotel on Friedrichstrasse. The rectangle, the right angle, and the circle are the basic elements of this project. Two cylindrical towers at the corners mediated between the acute and obtuse angles of the streets, and the terraced setbacks in Loos's project corresponded to the cornices and setbacks of the adjacent buildings. The two rectangular grids on the facade can be projected onto the grid of the plan. The axis of symmetry led from the subtractive volume of the entry, through the rectangular hall, to the semi-circular ballroom. This ingenious solution, while hierarchically ordering the spaces, allowed the architecture to absorb several undesirable deformations where the two grids met. The sobriety of the facades was achieved through the use of square, unrecessed fenestration, smooth surfaces, and exclusion of superfluous ornamentation. The architecture of this building is surprising in its extraordinary union of formal minimalism and transitional composition.

145a WINTER SPORTS RESORT, SEMMERING MOUNTAINS, 1913.
Perspective of court.

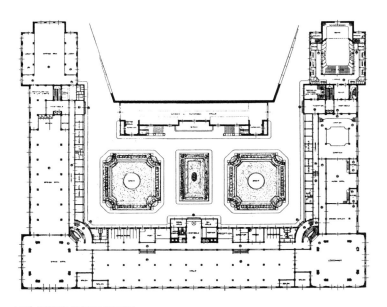

145b WINTER SPORTS RESORT.
Ground floor plan. Loos's rational, minimalist elevations are exercises in classical rigor.

146a GRAND HOTEL BABYLON, NICE, 1913.
Perspective.

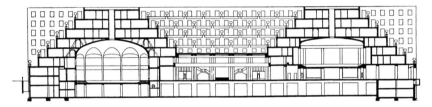

146b GRAND HOTEL BABYLON.
Section.

Released from the constraints of the urban context, Loos developed a hotel that respected canonical regularity. In 1921, participating in a competition "for the construction of a modern hotel" in Zagreb, he proposed a massive rectangular building. The original model and plans have disappeared; all that remains of this project are several sketches. The sketch of the ground floor (Fig. 144) is important for two reasons. First, it reveals a classical, almost Palladian composition of surprising purity and "clarity" (thus the name of the project—Hotel Clarté): a large circular room inscribed within a rectangular plan. Second, it illuminates a little-known facet of Loos's design process: the genesis of form. The sketch of the plan shows an initial grid of small squares divided in four. The relationship of 7:5 (1.4) between the two sides is clearly established. However, Loos seems to have wanted to lengthen one of the shorter sides (at the left, on the bottom, and on top) to make the project into a rectangle of 1.414—the square root of two—a proportion used by Vitruvius,

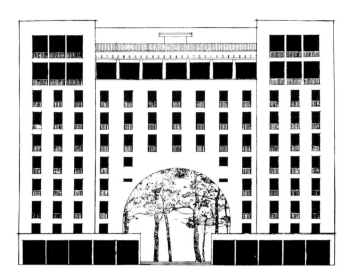

147 HOTEL, JUANS-LES-PINS, COTE D'AZUR, 1931.
Elevation. The high, arched opening allowed a view to the grove of pine trees.

Palladio, and in classical architecture in general. This allows us to speculate that Loos employed a nineteenth-century method for quickly determining the ideal measurements of a plan.[20]

One finds the same ordering system in Loos's proposals for a winter sports resort in the Semmering Mountains (Austria, 1913, Fig. 145) and for the Grand Hotel Babylon (Nice, 1910, Fig. 146), both shown at the Salon d'automne in 1923. Both projects were also variations on the U-shaped plan. For the Babylon, two ziggurat blocks were to rise from a low, massive base. Each bedroom was to have a terrace. Loos compared the project to two pyramids enclosing two giant sepulchral vaults, the vaults, in this case, being a skating rink and a grand ballroom. Natural light could filter down into both spaces through light wells in the center of each pyramid (Fig. 146b). With its exotic and worldly atmosphere, it would evoke both the hanging gardens of Semiramis and Hollywood, the modern Babylon.

The last hotel evaluated here fits only partially into the typology of the preceding buildings, but it illustrates three important aspects of Loos's design process: the role of site and context, indifference to originality, and liberal reference to historical precedent. Loos's project was a counterproposal, designed in 1931, to oppose the construction of a hotel in a pine grove in Juan-les-Pins on the French Riviera (Fig. 147).[21] Loos's vertical deployment of the

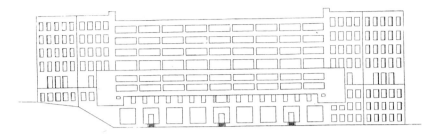

148 SCHWARZWALD SCHOOL, SEMMERING MOUNTAINS, 1911–1912.
North elevation. Loos maintained purist simplicity in the functional buildings he designed before the first world war.

building limited the destruction of the pine grove and permitted views of the latter from the street through a vaulted arch in the center of the facade. Axial progression—constant in all other of Loos's hotels—was sacrificed for the benefit of the natural environment. The restaurant and dance floor, usually situated centrally on the ground floor, were relocated to the top floor and onto the terrace in order "to have a view towards Cap d'Antibes and Cannes." Loos believed that this layout would create "an attraction for the whole coast."[22] He also declared to have looked to no "new idea"; he had designed his hotel "based on the already proven system of the Wilson Palace at Juan-les-Pins," believing that originality should always subordinate itself to utilitarian perfection. The unusual configuration of this hotel recalls a city gate by Boullée that Loos had admired in an illustrated article on "revo-lutionary" French architecture. His friend, Franz Gluck, had sent the article from Vienna while Loos was designing the hotel in Juan-les-Pins.[23] As attested to by a student, Kurt Unger, who collaborated on the project, Loos had made this comparison himself, all the while affirming that he had had *his* idea before seeing Boullée's drawing.[24] Still, it is impos-sible to trace the paternity of this, or any, idea. One must remember that Loos often worked from a palate of classical or traditional forms (the Pantheon in Rome, the mausoleum of Halicarnassus, ziggurats, and Doric columns, to name a few) for certain of his architectural schemes, without hesitating to displace their original functions for his own. From Boullée's city gate, the hotel at Juan-les-Pins retains only a memory of a triumphal arch and a refer-ence to the "revolutionary" period which, a century prior to Loos, had already influenced German neoclassicism.

Using the same logic, Loos proposed very similar projects for two buildings whose chance of being realized was quite unlikely. Stripped facades and U-shaped plans characterized two buildings that shared a context but not a function. One proposal was for a winter sports resort (Fig. 145), and the other was for the Schwarzwald School (1911–1912, Fig. 148), both in the

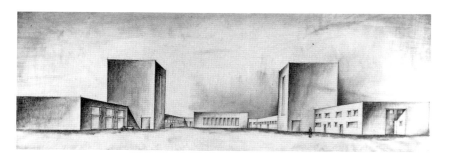

149 STABLES FOR PRINCE SANGUSZKO, SOUTH OF FRANCE (?), 1924.
Frontal perspective.

Semmering Mountains. The composition of the school was based, like that of the hotel, on the symmetry of the plan and the volumes. The walls were of a smooth surface, consistent with the conceptual transparency of an architecture purified of all useless ornament.

Loos's proposal for Prince Sanguszko's stables (planned for the South of France, 1924, Fig. 149) was remarkably similar to his earlier design for a commemorative monument to the Emperor Franz-Josef in Vienna (Fig. 135), although more in perspectival effect than in volumetric disposition. The same U-shaped plan governs these two otherwise different projects. The buildings differ in external treatment; the severity of the functional building is clearly opposed to the classical decorum of the commemorative monument. Loos felt that a utilitarian building such as a stables required no adornment, whereas a commemorative monument owed, in great part, its ostentatious character to the addition of decorative elements: expressive garments to clothe the volumes. However, the bareness of the stables did not necessarily denote a modern approach, as the composition was attached more to classicism than to a purist aesthetic derived from cubism.

The last utilitarian building to evaluate is a large office building complete with a cinema, which Loos worked on while in Paris in 1925 (Fig. 150). It was to occupy the whole of a traffic island bounded by the Boulevard des Italiens and the rues Louis-le-Grand, Michodière, and Hanovre. Aligning his building with these streets and respecting the confines and angles of the site, Loos proposed a tower of nearly fifty meters (165 feet) high, which would have dominated the boulevard like an American skyscraper. Loos considered the reciprocity between the building and its context at two levels: subordinating the building to its context to safeguard urban continuity, while still providing a distinctive and identifiable symbol. The top floor of Loos's building (a luxurious restaurant) was to be ringed by ionic columns so that the tower could be perceived and recognized from afar.

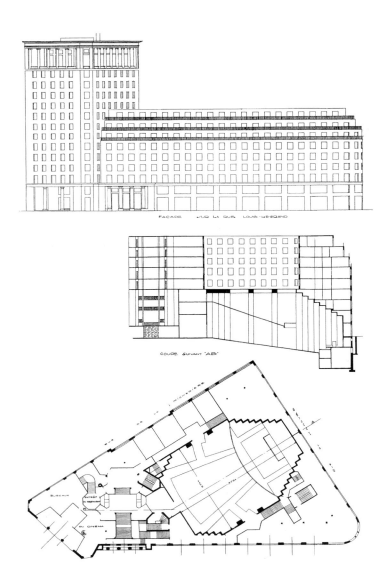

150 OFFICE BUILDING AND CINEMA, BOULEVARD DES ITALIENS, PARIS, 1925.
Boulevard des Italiens/rue Louis-le-Grand elevation, section, ground floor plan.

Despite the supposed resemblance between the facades of Loos's utilitarian buildings and those of the Modern Movement, there lies a profound difference, a formal, and even an ethical misunderstanding. What the avant-garde modernists presented as a void or absence of language, representing their break with the past, Loos saw as the outcome of a secular tradition. Apart from some additional and structurally superfluous columns, the austere configuration of his office building on the Boulevard des Italiens was based on the logic of a "return to reason" (*wieder zur Besinnung gekommen*) which, in Loos's opinion, enjoyed a rejuvenation in France in the 1920s, with the appearance of a "modern classicism" exemplified by the work of Auguste Perret.[25]

CHAPTER SEVEN
LOOS'S ARCHITECTURE: ELEMENTS OF ANALYSIS

At the beginning of this century, Loos succeeding in uniting, more in his critical positions than in his architecture, reason and nature, ethics and aesthetics, and classicism and the vernacular. He followed a solitary route, indifferent to the avant-garde and estranged from both the Viennese Secession and the International Style. Obstinately reverent of the classical masters and yet open to the most audacious and radical ideas, he sought an architecture which, in the name of achieving the "best," resisted the ideology of "new." "A change with regard to tradition is only permissible if the change means an improvement."[1] He believed that beauty resided in the perfection of the object, or in the object's finality. Was he a functionalist? He did take care to maintain that form must follow function, but "Of course, the functional object by itself is not beautiful," he wrote in 1898, in one of his first essays; "There is more to it than that."[2] For the definition of this supplement, an aesthetic one, he looked to Leon Battista Alberti: "An object that is so perfect that one can neither add to it nor take away from it without harming it is beautiful."[3] Loos derived this classical conception of beauty from his German and Austrian ancestors: Gottfried Semper and Otto Wagner.[4]

Loos often contested the sterile imitation of past styles, but he also felt that an individual was incapable of inventing new forms. He saw creation as the result of a continuum of unconscious, multi-generational, collective work. For Loos, the essence of architecture did not reveal genius, but rather the knowledge and mastery of craft and construction, as well as an acceptance of the necessity for a sort of anonymity. By refusing formal innovation, Loos was led to propose his distillation of elements tested by the classical tradition and by English and American culture. Symmetry, regularity of contours, tripartite axial plans, columns, and porticos reappeared in his projects alongside his exposed brick fireplaces and false wood beams, together creating the art of modern building (*Baukunst*) and a universally recognized language.[5]

There are four basic points essential to Loos's ideas on composition: the *visible surface*, the *material structure*, the *space-volume*, and *finality*.[6] The visible surface conveys a building's image. As with light and color, it concerns all that belongs to the visible realm. It is the thin membrane that clads the walls of both the interior and the exterior of the building, and thus constitutes its "facades." The material structure is the skeleton of the building (beams, columns, brick, steel, stone, etc.): the technological underpinnings of its existence, usually concealed, although sometimes revealed (in the case of the Looshaus for example, Fig. 115). The space-volume is the form circumscribed by the material structure on the inside and outside of the buildings. Lastly, the finality designates the emotional and functional component of the building, and its social and psychological purpose.

These four notions can be ordered in two opposed series. The first series describes the *perception* of the completed building: one sees the visible surface, one interprets the material structure, one defines the space-volume, and one identifies the finality. The second describes the *conception* of the building, reversing the perceptual order: finality, space-volume, material structure, visible surface. Together, the two series define the Loosian system of composition: *conception* with consideration of *perception*. This breakdown of the design process is conditioned by a fundamental paradox between public and private, monument and house, and exteriors and interiors of buildings.

The tension between public and private is the basis of Loos's design methodology. To design a house, the essence of the private realm, it is necessary to familiarize oneself with the needs and habits of the occupants, then develop an arrangement of spaces linked to their lifestyles. The required space-volumes are then defined by the material structure and technological skeleton. It remains only to produce the visible surface.

Although on the exterior, Loos's facades tend towards inexpression, the interior visible surface is richly decorated to conform to the personal taste of the inhabitants, even if it is "bad taste." For Loos these interiors, skillfully "decorated" with geometrically artistic materials, were not created for passersby. Their perception of the building need not extend beyond the simple recognition that "this here is a house," a house that reveals nothing of the character or status of its occupants. "Let one house look like the other!" wrote Loos in 1914, considering that this similarity was the best way to serve "one's time, oneself and one's people and humanity well. And by that, one's native country!"[7]

Conversely, Loos believed that monuments and civic buildings ought to belong to everyone, to be viewed by all, to be *signs* with explicit finality. The workings of the interior were not discernible from the exterior; there was no *transparency*. The exterior form—the visible surface—alone expressed and symbolized the unseen function. The passerby could understand the function merely by viewing the exterior, which conveyed the true power of the State and its ideological apparatus.

Loos ordered his public buildings based on their context. One could say that however rigidly ordered the spaces of these projects may seem, their overall volumes are analogous to the Raumplan. In contrast to his residences, in the public buildings, the Raumplan is perceptible contextually. The urban space, like a mold, becomes the material structure that informs the space-volume of the entire building.

Loos created beautifully rendered perspectives that showed his projects in their context, accenting the perception of the city while neutralizing the interior of the buildings. The plan for a multi-story type, such as the *Chicago Tribune* tower, is determined by the exterior form of the building (Fig. 151): a simple, neutral, rational, and functional division of an inflexible circle.

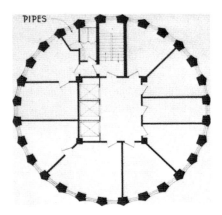

151   *CHICAGO TRIBUNE* COMPETITION ENTRY.
Typical floor plan.

In a brilliant statement published in 1913, Karl Kraus, the Viennese moralist, summed up the duality of Loos's work in relation to culture. In defending Loos's statement that a house is not a monument, nor a monument a house, he wrote "Adolf Loos and I, he in reality, I verbally, have nothing else to do but to show that there is a difference between an urn and a chamber pot and that this difference is necessary because it guarantees the game of culture. The others, on the other hand, the defenders of 'positive' values, divide themselves between those who take an urn for a chamber pot and those who take the chamber pot for an urn."[8]

CHAPTER EIGHT
THE BIBLIOGRAPHY OF ADOLF LOOS:
AN AMBIGUOUS POSTERITY

To be interested in Loos, to refer to his writings, his projects, and his built work, has become a necessity, almost an reflex, in the last fifteen years. The republication of his texts in Austria and Germany (1962) and their subsequent translation into several languages, the numerous articles on him, often by premier authors,[1] the exhaustive monographs on his life and work,[2] and the international exhibition and colloquium organized by the French Institute of Architecture in 1983 are all proof of Loos's growing topicality.

In the reception we have given him and in the texts dedicated to him, the divisive issue, as we have seen, is the question of modernism. Was he a pioneer of the Modern Movement or of the postmodern controversy? The response to this question varies according to the date of publication of each particular book or essay. The first wave of critics saluted Loos as the precursor to the purism of the 1920s and 1930s.[3] For these authors, his architecture revealed above all else the visible: simple geometric volumes, flat roofs, smooth white surfaces, absence of ornament on the facade, and windows that were large and usually lacked frames. These critics cite Loos's houses and villas, and his renovations of stores and cafes, but never mention his urban projects or his public buildings and monuments. The garden facade of the Steiner House (Fig. 60) is the typical reference, as it embodies the qualities most compatible with modern architectural history. This limited view of Loos's significance weakens in the 1960s and tends to disappear by the 1970s and 1980s.

A "new vision" was adopted at the end of the 1950s, which blossomed twenty years later. The new reading of Loos's work revolved around questions of language and significance. His writings found new favor among a more disparate group of architects who viewed his built work, projects, and sketches in entirety, acknowledging and even welcoming the stylistic contradictions. The new approach depended principally on the reading of the work; the same formal elements were considered an expression of rational steps, putting concept *before* form.[4] The Steiner House remained an example and a masterpiece, but became even more in that its forms were seen as beautiful, not only in spite of themselves, but as components of a larger whole of complex and ingenious concepts and rules of composition. As a result, many previously ignored works—those that contradicted the formal principles of the Modern Movement—resurfaced. The use of classical or traditional elements was no longer considered taboo. The second wave of critics recognized an *architecture parlante* in the iconographically rich, contextual, and historic nature of Loos's urban projects.

This "new Loos," a multi-faceted figure, appears as a critic of contemporary architecture and urbanism,[5] one whose work reflects the ambiguities of his critical stance. The ambiguities are born of an implicit tension in program (interior/exterior, private/public, house/monument, ornamentation/decoration). The work is coherent, but its coherence is often evasive, not apparent on the first "reading." The readings of Loos's work, like so many of the "writings" on it, are contradictory. Yet these contradictions seem appropriate, or at least understandable, and in the end, reinforce the work.

Very few books were written about Loos during his lifetime. The first two, Karl Marilaun, *Adolf Loos* (Vienna and Leipzig, 1922; Czech translation: Brno, 1929) and Bohuslav Markalous, *Adolf Loos* (Prague, 1929), are somewhat limited in scope.

The first definitive volume, *Adolf Loos, Das Werk des Architekten* (Vienna, 1931), was written by Heinrich Kulka, Loos's student and partner. For a long time, this work remained an indispensible reference because of its numerous reproductions of plans and photographs (270 in all), most published for the first time. Until then, Loos had owed his principle renown—outside of Vienna—to his polemical writings. The architects and artists who sought his advice, in Paris for example, knew almost nothing of his architectural work. Also in 1931, Éditions Crès, Paris published a small book by Franz Gluck: *Adolf Loos*. Although brief, it did contain thirty-two photogravure reproductions of Loos's interiors and houses.

After Loos's death the monographs can be divided into two groups. The first, prevalent until the 1970s, strove to make known his life and work. The second, and more enduring, is more retrospective in nature, consistent with the "rediscovery" of Loos.

Section One

In Vienna, 1936, Loos's fourth and last wife published a book on his life: Claire Loos, *The Private Adolf Loos*. In 1947, also in Vienna, his first wife, Lina Loos, wrote *Das Buch ohne Titel, Erlebte Geschichten*. Nine years later, Ludwig Münz, a friend of Loos's who had conserved his archives—now located at the Graphische Sammlung Albertina of Vienna—published a monograph that included new iconographic elements: *Adolf Loos* (Milan, 1956). This first Italian publication helped contribute to Loos's renown in that country and launched, twenty-three years after his death, a broad debate on his architecture.

In 1960, Oskar Kokoschka (1886–1980), a close friend of Loos's, received the Érasme Prize (with Marc Chagall). Loyal to the memory of Loos, to whom he owed his first encouragement, he dedicated his prize to the creation of a monograph that would help illuminate Loos's work, most of which was still unknown to the general public. After Münz died in 1957, Gustav Kunstler took up this task, continuing Münz's efforts.[6] Kunstler, who had been able to access Loos's archives, then held by Maria Münz, in 1964 published a remarkable study that included the first catalog of Loos's works. He included his own essays, as well as those Münz had written in 1956, thus the dual authorship: Ludwig Münz, Gustav Kunstler, *Der Architekt Adolf Loos* (Vienna and Munich, 1964). An English translation, with a new introduction by Nicholas Pevsner and commentary by Oskar Kokoschka, appeared two years later: *Adolf Loos: Pioneer of Modern Architecture* (London, New York, and Washington, 1966). Accessible for the first time in English—excepting the occasional cursory reference to Loos in architectural history texts—his work was finally revealed to a larger public.

Concurrently, Loos's two written pieces were republished in one volume under the direction of Franz Gluck, another friend of the architect: *Adolf Loos, samtliche Schriften*, t. I (Vienna and Munich, 1962). Finally, another book of memoirs appeared several years later, written by Loos's third wife: Elsie Altmann-Loos, *Adolf Loos, der Mensch* (Vienna and Munich, 1968). In 1961, the first exhibition on Loos since World War II took place in Vienna at the Wurthle gallery. With the generous cooperation of Maria Münz, the gallery was able to present several original pieces from the Münz archives.

Section Two

In November 1959, only three years after the appearance of Münz's book in Italy, the Milan architectural review *Casabella-continuità*, directed by Ernesto Rogers, dedicated an entire issue, Number 233, to Loos. This special issue, which Rogers entitled "The Reality of Adolf Loos," was conceived by Aldo Rossi, an architect born the year that Loos had died. Rossi republished an important essay in which he reinterpreted the work of the Viennese architect.

This Italian theoretical reevaluation was followed by G. Perugini, *Perche Loos* (Rome, 1970), the Italian translation of Loos's two books: *Parole nel vuoto, Nonostante tutto*, introduction by Joseph Rykwert (Milan, 1972), F. Amendolagine, M. Cacciari, *Oikos: da Loos a Wittgenstein* (Rome, 1975), M. Cacciari, *Adolf Loos e il suo Angelo*, followed by a facsimile of *Das Andere*, Loos's publication, the translation of *Festschrift zum 60. Geburstag/Per i sesant'anni di Adolf Loos* (Milan, 1981), and finally, an ambitious yet insufficient publication, one which claimed to be the ultimate Loosian volume: Benedetto Gravagnuolo, *Adolf Loos, Theory and Works*, introduction by Aldo Rossi (Milan, 1982).

If the Italians were actively interested in Loos's "rationalism," the Austrians focused on analyses and historic syntheses, most of which were published in the 1970s and 1980s. The first, by Hermann Czech and Wolfgang Mistelbauer: *Das Looshaus, eine Monographie* (Vienna, 1976), was a remarkable study on the Looshaus. It was followed by Burkhardt

Rukschcio and Roland Schachel's, *Adolf Loos, Leben und Werk* (Salzburg and Vienna, 1982; French edition: Brussels and Liège, 1987), an enormous monograph, the result of a meticulously thorough archival study which provides, for the first time, a systematic catalog of Loos's work.

Loos's writings were republished in Vienna in three volumes (1981, 1982, 1983), under the direction of Adolf Opel. The third volume, *Die Potemkinsche Stadt*, reunites the texts that Loos had excluded from his two collections, and the two other volumes reissue the original editions of *Ins Leere gesprochen* and *Trotzdem*. In the same manner, the inaugural work by Heinrich Kulka was republished in Vienna in 1979 and 1985, as were the memoirs by Claire Loos (1985), and those of Lina Loos and Elsie Altmann-Loos (*Mein Leben mit Adolf Loos*, 1986).

The catalog *Adolf Loos* was published on the occasion of an important exhibition in Vienna (December 1989–February 1990) in which the leaders of the Austrian architectural community participated. The catalog included many previously unpublished pieces on Loos's work and life.

The proliferation of Loosian studies was most prevalent in Italy and Austria. Nevertheless, the following publications merit mention. Mihaly Kubinszky, *Adolf Loos* (Budapest, 1967; German translation: Berlin, 1970) is the most notable monograph. The others are translations of Loos's writings into Spanish, French, Italian, and English, respectively: Adolf Loos, *Ornamento y delito, y otros escritos* (Barcelona, 1972), edited and introduced by R. Schachel, Adolf Loos, *Paroles dans le vide. Malgré tout* (Paris, 1979), Adolf Loos, *La civiltà oddidentale*, "Das Andere" *e altri scritti* (1981), introduction by Aldo Rossi, and Adolf Loos, *Spoken into the Void: Collected Essays 1897–1900* (Cambridge, MA and London, 1982), introduction by Aldo Rossi.

Finally, it is interesting to note the resurgence of French interest in Loos's work, which led to a 1983 exhibition in Paris organized by the French Institute of Architecture in collaboration with an international colloquium. The exhibit reunited most of the authors mentioned in this section. The exhibit and colloquium are recorded in a catalog entitled *Adolf Loos, 1870–1933* (Liège and Brussels, 1983).

NOTES

Chapter One

1   See the introduction by Nikolaus Pevsner to the English edition of L. Münz and G. Kunstler, *Adolf Loos: Pioneer of Modern Architecture* (New York: Praeger, 1966).

2   Talbot Hamlin, *Greek Revival Architecture in America* (New York, 1944).

3   R. Musil, "L'homme allemand comme symptôme," French translation, *L'Énergumène*, no. 5 (1975), p. 10. One can muse about the role that men like Otto Wagner, Gustav Mahler and Aloïs Riegl each played within their respective fields.

4   Ibid., p. 12.

5   J. Bouveresse, "Les derniers jours de l'humanité," *Critique*, no. 339–340 (1975), p. 785.

6   With this term we designate groups of artists who, at the turn of the century in Munich, Berlin, and Vienna, broke with academic art. The painter Gustav Klimt and the architects Joseph Hoffmann and Josef-Maria Olbrich were among the eminent personalities of the Viennese Secession, created in 1897.

7   A. Loos, "Potemkin City (July 1898)," in *Spoken into the Void: Collected Essays 1897–1900*, translated by Jane O. Newman and John H. Smith (Cambridge, MA: MIT Press, 1982), p. 95.

8   "Who does not know of Potemkin's villages, the ones that Catherine's cunning favorite built in the Ukraine? They were villages of canvas and pasteboard, villages intended to transform a visual desert into a flowering landscape for the eyes of Her Imperial Majesty....Surely such things are only possible in Russia! But the Potemkin city of which I wish to speak here is none other than our dear Vienna herself." Ibid.

9   Ibid, pp. 95–96.

10   A. Loos, "Postscript (1910)," to "Ornament and Crime (1908)." As a general rule, the dates that accompany the titles (within the quotation marks) are those of Loos himself. They indicate the date of the manuscript's drafting, not its publication date.

11   Certain Viennese cafes (Cafe Griensteidl or Cafe Central) were meeting places for writers and intellectuals; they functioned as forums where critical questions of creation were debated. Among its habitués, the Cafe Central counted Kraus, Altenberg, and Loos. The threesome had a regular table.

12   This concert of works of the new Viennese school provoked violent public reaction. There were incidents and even a lawsuit. See Mosco Carner's French translation of *Alban Berg* (Paris, 1979), p. 52.

13   A. Loos, "Ladies' Fashion (August 21 1898)," in *Spoken into the Void*, op, cit., p. 99.

14   A. Loos, "Mon école d'architecture (1913)," in *Malgré tout* (Paris, 1979), pp. 231–232.

15   Ibid., p. 232.

16   B. Michel, "Adolf Loos et la société austro-hongroise avant 1914," *Adolf Loos 1870–1933*, catalog to the 1983 exhibition at the Institute of French Architecture (Liège and Brussels), p. 62.

17   A. Loos, "Ornement et éducation (1924)," in *Malgré tout*, op. cit., p. 290.

18   O. Kokoschka, *Ma Vie* (1971), French translation (Paris, 1986), p. 76; see also his preface to L. Münz, G. Kunstler, *Adolf Loos: Pioneer of Modern Architecture*, op. cit., p. 11.

19   Homage by Tristan Tzara in *Adolf Loos Festschrift zum 60. Gebrustag* (Vienna, 1930), not paginated.

20   Homage by Stephen Zweig in *Adolf Loos Festschrift zum 60. Gebrustag*, op. cit.

21   A. Loos, "Architecture (1910)," in *The Architecture of Adolf Loos* (British Arts Council exhibition catalog, 1985) p. 108.

Chapter Two

1   A. Loos, "Foreword," in *Spoken into the Void*, op. cit., p. 2.

2   See notes 7, 8, and 9 of chapter one. This short pamphlet, published in the Secession's news organ, announced the criticism of ornament formulated by Loos in "Ornament and Crime." The great success of this last text in the 1920s without doubt supported the inclusion of "Potemkin City" in the second edition of *Spoken into the Void*.

3   Academic society for literature and music.

4   Bibliographic note by F. Gluck, Loos's friend and partner, who republished his text in 1962.

5   A. Loos, "Ornament and Crime (1908)," in *Adolf Loos: Pioneer of Modern Architecture*, op. cit., pp. 226–227.

6   A. Loos, "Ornement e éducation (1924)," in *Malgré tout*, op. cit., p. 289.

7   "When man is born, his instincts are those of a new-born dog. His childhood runs through all the changes corresponding to the history of mankind. At the age of two he looks like a Papuan, at four like one of an ancient Germanic tribe, at six like Socrates, at eight like Voltaire....The Papuan tattoos his skin, his boat, his rudder, his oars; in short, everything he can get his hands on. He is no criminal.

The modern man who tattoos himself is a criminal or a degenerate....The urge to decorate one's face and everything in reach is the origin of the graphic arts....But what is natural for a Papuan and a child, is degenerate for modern man." Adolf Loos, "Ornament and crime (1908)," in *Adolf Loos: Pioneer of Modern Architecture*, op. cit., p. 226.

8   A. Loos, "Ornement et éducation (1924)," op. cit., p. 289.

9   A. Loos, "Ladies' Fashion (August 21, 1898)," in *Spoken into the Void*, op. cit., p. 99.

10   M. Tafuri, F. Dal Co, *Architettura contemporanea* (Milan, 1976), chapter 7.

11   A. Loos, "Architecture (1910)," in *The Architecture of Adolf Loos*, op. cit. p. 104. The remainder of the quotations in this chapter are also taken from this article.

12   "The house has to please everyone, contrary to the work of art, which does not. The work of art is a private matter for the artist. The house is not. The work of art is brought into the world without there being a need for it. The house satisfies a requirement. The work of art is responsible to none; the house is responsible to everyone. The work of art wants to draw people out of their state of comfort. The house has to serve comfort. The work of art is revolutionary; the house is conservative. The work of art shows people new directions and thinks of the future. The house thinks of the present. Man loves everything that satisfies his comfort. He hates everything that wants to draw him out of his acquired and secured position and that disturbs him. Thus he loves the house and hates art." Ibid., p. 107–108.

13   Loos speaks here in very broad terms. In actuality, he insisted on a contrast between the private zone and the public domain (chapter 4).

Chapter Three

1   A. Loos, excerpts from "Das Andere," (1903), in *Malgré tout*, op. cit., p. 172.

2   Ibid., p. 173.

3   A. Loos, "The Poor Little Rich Man (April 26, 1900)," in *Spoken into the Void*, op. cit., p. 125.

4   A. Loos, "Das Andere" (1903), op. cit., p. 173.

5   The houses by the American architect Henry Hobson Richardson (1838–1886) allied a highly functional asymmetrical layout with a decorative use of raw materials stripped of ornament. Richardson, who spent two years at the École des Beaux Arts in Paris, proposed a specifically American equilibrium between contemporary ideas from England and France. His work profoundly affected the architects of the Chicago School and Frank Lloyd Wright. See Henry-Russell Hitchcock,

H.H. Richardson and His Time (New York, 1936) and Jeffrey Karl Ochsner, *H.H. Richardson, Complete Architectural Works* (Cambridge, MA, 1982).

6   R. Neutra, *Amerika-Kie Stilbildung des neues Bauens in den Vereinigten Staaten* (Vienna, 1930), pp. 44–45.

7   A. Loos, "Josef Veillich (1929)," in *Malgré tout*, op. cit., pp. 323–324.

8   H. Kulka, *Adolf Loos* (Vienna, 1931), p. 42.

9   A. Loos, "The Christmas Exhibition at the Austrian Museum (December 18, 1897)," in *Spoken into the Void*, op. cit., p. 94.

10   A. Loos, "Architecture (1910)," in *The Architecture of Adolf Loos*, op. cit., p. 107.

11   N. Pevsner, *Pioneers of Modern Design, from William Morris to Walter Gropius* (1936) (Harmondsworth, 1975), p. 199.

12   "The bright red lacquered chair with yellow wickerwork that seems so terribly English to us today...can be found in numerous pictures of German interiors from the eighteenth century, especially those by Chodowiecki." A. Loos, "The Christmas Exhibition at the Austrian Museum (December 18, 1897)," in *Spoken into the Void*, op. cit., pp. 92–93.

13   *Fremden-Blatt* (Vienna, November 22, 1907).

14   H. Kulka, op. cit., p. 29.

15   A. Loos, "Review of the Arts and Crafts (October 1, 1898)," in *Spoken into the Void*, op. cit., p. 104.

16   Ibid., p. 105.

17   O. Kokoschka, *Ma vie*, op. cit., p. 78 (revised translation).

18   *Fremden-Blatt* (Vienna, November 22, 1907).

19   A. Loos, "Hands Off! (1917)," in *Malgré tout*, op. cit., pp. 249–250.

20   A. Loos, "The Principle of Cladding (September 4, 1898)," in *Spoken into the Void*, op. cit., p. 67.

Chapter Four

1   One does not see here the number of important sketches of houses or quickly abandoned fragmentary projects, several of which were remarkable.

2   A. Loos, "Sur la maison de la Michaelerplatz (1910)," in *Malgré tout*, op. cit., p. 213.

3   A. Loos, "Mon école d'architecture (1913)," in *Malgré tout*, op. cit., p. 233.

4   A. Loos, "Les cités ouvrières modernes (1926)," in *Malgré tout*, op. cit., p. 309.

5   A. Loos, "Vernacular Art (1914)," in *The Architecture of Adolf Loos*, op. cit., pp. 110–113.

6   For Loos, classical architecture drew its sources from antiquity. Its rules of composition and its decorative elements form a tradition which, from the Renaissance in Rome on, became a common language to Western civilization. In this sense it is impossible to restrict classicism to a restrained spatial and temporal context: the value of the classical spirit, eternally present, crosses modern times from the Renaissance to the Baroque, from Fischer von Erlach and from Schinkel to Gottfried Semper, Otto Wagner, and Loos himself (see A. Loos, *Spoken into the Void*, op. cit.). See, on the other hand, J. Summerson, *Le langage classique de l'architecture* (1963), (French trans., Paris, 1981); A. Tzonis, L. Lefaivre, D. Bilodeau, *Le classicisme en architecture: la poétique de l'ordre* (1983), (French trans., Paris, 1985).

7   A. Loos, "Potemkin City (July 1898)," in *Spoken into the Void*, op. cit.

8   A. Loos, "Ornement e éducation (1924)," in *Malgré tout*, op. cit., p. 232.

9   A. Loos, "Mon école d'architecture (1913)," op. cit., p. 232.

10   A. Loos, "Ornement e éducation (1924)," op. cit., pp. 289–290; see also chapter 2, p. 27.

11   A. Loos, "Ornement e éducation (1924)," op. cit., p. 290.

12   Ibid.

13   A. Loos, "Vernacular Art (1914)," in *The Architecture of Adolf Loos*, op. cit., p. 113.

14   The term *Raumplan* was introduced by Heinrich Kulka, who, in his book of 1931, gave the first detailed description of this method of composition, developed by his mentor (translation from French): "Thanks to Loos, a new and more elaborate conception of space became known to the world: the realization of thought in space, the composition of plans that consist of many different levels, the composition of different pieces that still relate to each other to create a harmonious structure based on the economy of space. The pieces have, according to location and use, not only varying sizes but varying heights. Loos could, by this method, create a greater quantity of habitable space in the same volume, on the same site, under the same roof, between the same walls [as another architect not designing by this method], by using a greater number of individual spaces. He exploits, maximally, the possibilities offered by the material and the habitable volume. To phrase it in another manner: the architect who thinks only horizontally needs to construct a larger space to create the same habitable volume [as Loos]. In these houses the halls are unnecessarily long, the space less rentable, the value reduced;

construction of such a house would be a burden and would mean higher costs all around." H. Kulka, *Adolf Loos*, op. cit., p. 14.

15   A. Loos, "Josef Veillich (1929)," in *Malgré tout*, op. cit., p. 323 (translation from French): "The great architectural revolution is the resolution of the plan in space! Before Emmanuel Kant, man could not think spatially and architects were constrained to make bathrooms with ceilings as high as the rest of the rooms. In reducing their height by half, they could better accommodate the spaces below or above. Just as man will, one day, be able to image space as volume, other architects will be able to resolve the plan in space." See also Max Risselada (ed.), *Raumplan versus Plan Libre, Adolf Loos and Le Corbusier* (New York, 1988).

16   A. Loos, "Apprendre à habiter (1921)," in *Malgré tout*, op. cit., pp. 279–280.

17   A. Loos, "Interiors in the Rotunda (June 12, 1898)," in *Spoken into the Void*, op. cit., pp. 23–27.

18   See this letter in B. Rukschcio, B. Schachel, *Adolf Loos* (Brussels and Liège, 1987), p. 327.

19   A. Loos, "Vernacular Art (1914)," in *The Architecture of Adolf Loos*, op. cit., p. 111.

20   A. Loos, "Sur la maison de la Michaelerplatz (1910)," op. cit., p. 211. Vitruvius advised architects to (translation from French) "make the best possible use of materials. Architects should employ materials that can be found and prepared at a reasonable cost; there are places where one can not find good sand, nor good stone, nor [l'abies], nor fir trees, nor marble, where one must, to have these things, have them brought from afar at great inconvenience and expense." *Les Dix Livres de l'architecture*, I, 5, translation by Claude Perrault reviewed by Andre Dalmas (Paris, 1979), p. 33.

21   A. Loos, "Das Grand-Hotel Babylon," *Die Neue Wirtschaft*, December 20, 1923. Reprinted in A. Loos, *Die potemkinsche Stadt* (Vienna, 1983), p. 197.

22   "It was only this summer," wrote Loos in 1914, "that the construction of a family house in Hietzing was rejected by the committee, according to the minutes, with the following words: 'The facade is wanting in picturesque arrangements, as is the custom in this area by applying roofs, small turrets, gables and bay windows. On the grounds of these shortcomings, the building license is not granted.'" A. Loos, "Vernacular Art (1914)," in *The Architecture of Adolf Loos*, op. cit. p. 112.

23   A. Loos, "Vernacular Art (1914)," in *The Architecture of Adolf Loos*, op.cit.

24   A. Loos, "Das Grand-Hotel Babylon," op. cit., pp. 197–198.

25   J. Hambridge, *Dynamic Symmetry* (New Haven, CT, 1920), pp. 25–26, pp. 197–198; see also M. Ghyka, *Esthétique des proportions dans la nature et dans les arts* (Paris, 1927 and 1988), plate 62.

26   French translation, *Rien qu'un rêve* (Paris, 1953).

27   The plan of the house of Margarethe Stoneborough-Wittgenstein (Vienna, 1926–1928) was con-

ceived by Paul Engelmann. But it was mostly the philosopher Ludwig Wittgenstein, the younger brother of the owner, who led the construction to completion by using Engelmann's plan to support an intellectual creation in space. See B. Leitner, *The Architecture of L. Wittgenstein* (Halifax, 1973) and F. Amendolagine, M. Cacciari, *Oikos-da Loos a Wittgenstein* (Rome, 1975).

28   See the interpretation of the Viennese historian Emil Kaufmann, *Von Ledous bis Le Corbusier, Ursprung und Entwicklung der autonomen Architektur* (Vienna, 1933).

29   A. Loos, "Régles pour celui qui construi dans les montagnes (1913)," in *Malgré tout*, op. cit., pp. 236–237.

Chapter Five

1   A. Loos, "Architecture (1910)," in *The Architecture of Adolf Loos*, op. cit., p. 108.

2   A. Loos, "Sur la maison de la Michaelerplatz (1910)," in *Malgré tout*, op. cit., pp. 215–216.

3   Ibid., p. 217.

4   K. Kraus, *Die Fackel*, no. 313–314. Republished in H. Czech, W. Mistelbauer, *Das Looshaus* (Vienna, 1976), p. 84.

5   See the analysis by H. Czech, W. Mistelbauer, *Das Looshaus*, op. cit.

6   Gottfried Semper's fundamental work, *Der Stil in den technischen und tektonischen Künsten oder praktische Aesthetik* (vol. I: Frankfurt-on-Main, 1860; vol. II: Munich, 1863), was central, around 1900, to discussions in Otto Wagner's circle of acquaintances. The latter proposed, in his *Moderne Architektur* (Vienna, 1895), a definition of the architect based on the "Semperian model." We know that for Semper the beginnings of architecture coincide with that of textiles. In his view, the partition is the architectural element which formally offers closed space to the spirit. On the other hand, the framework and elements that carry this enclosure are a consequence that is foreign to the original architectural idea. For more on Semper's theory, see Wolfgang Hermann, Gottfried Semper, *In Search of Architecture* (Cambridge, MA, 1985), and Joseph Rykwert, "Gottfried Semper et la question du style," *Macula*, no. 5/6 (1979), pp. 176–189.

7   Loos lived in a town linked to the birth of history and to the theory of art, with Aloïs Riegl, Franz Wickhoff, Max Dvorak, etc. Their ideas were certainly an influence, even indirectly, on the history and cultural idea of architecture. We should remember Loos's mausoleum project for Max Dvorak (fig. 7), which evoked the tomb of Halicarnassus.

8   A. Loos, "Les cités ouvrières modernes (1926)," in *Malgré tout*, op. cit., pp. 295–314.

9   Loos explained the disadvantages of sunlight in the following way (translated from French): "We know that the sun is the worst enemy of the garden. The sun has produced much damage. The most magnificent and paradisiacal countries, from Mesopotamia to Syria and Egypt and all of North Africa, are victims of the sun. They have become arid. But the Arabs knew to find a solution to this situation: [they looked to] the Orient, where there exist gardening cultures in which the gardens are surrounded by walls to protect them from the wind and from the rays of the sun. What should our gardener do? He should surround his garden with a wall like this." Ibid., p. 300.

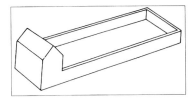

10   Ibid., p. 306.

11   "The high cost of construction materials and construction, together with the necessity to combat the great lack of housing, make it urgent to keep construction costs as low as possible, especially in the case of buildings for whom speed and economy are essential, as long as durability is of secondary importance. If the cost of the land, the construction materials, and the construction itself remain constant, economical construction is only possible if one limits the amount of material and work to be done. There exist well-known methods for this, such as the omission of attics and cellars. The invention in question [construction 'with a wall'] permits even more economy, on foundations, which are relatively expensive." A. Loos, "Das Haus mit einer Mauer," description of patent (February 11, 1921), reprinted from *Die potemkinsche Stadt*, op. cit., p. 181.

12   A. Loos, "Les cités ouvrières modernes (1926)," op. cit., p. 312.

13   Ibid., pp. 313–314.

Chapter Six

1   A. Rossi, "Adolf Loos, 1870–1933," *Casabella-Continuità*, no. 293 (1959); *L'Architettura della città* (Padua, 1966).

2   C. Sitte, *Städtebau nach seinen künstlerischen Grundsätzen* (Vienna, 1889).

3   B. Rukschcio, "Le plan de Vienne. Les travaux d'urbanisme d'Adolf Loos," *Adolf Loos 1870–1933*, op. cit., pp. 39–58.

4   A. Loos, "Vernacular Art (1914)," in *The Architecture of Adolf Loos*, op. cit., pp. 110–113.

5   These two statements about the rapport between art and architecture belong to Loos; see chapter two and A. Loos, "Architecture (1910)," in *The Architecture of Adolf Loos*, op. cit., pp. 104–109.

6   A. Loos, "Architecture (1910)," in *The Architecture of Adolf Loos*, op. cit., pp. 108.

7   Ibid.

8   A. Loos, "Quel est le plus beau...? (1907)," in *Malgré tout*, op. cit., pp. 186–187.

9   Remember that Loos's private houses were generally conceived in the inverse sense, from the interior to the exterior (see above, p. 67, and in this book, refer to chapter seven).

10   B. Rukschcio, R. Schachel, *Adolf Loos...*, op. cit., p. 454.

11   A. Loos, "The Principle of Cladding (September 4, 1898)," in *Spoken into the Void*, op. cit., p. 66.

12   The Ring (*Ringstrasse*) of Vienna is a vast complex of public buildings and homes aligned along a circular artery separating the old city from the suburbs. The Ring, built in the second half of the nineteenth century, occupied the place where the ancient city walls, now demolished, once stood. The grand isolated buildings, of a variety of styles and all facing the artery (the only cohesive element), reflected the highest values of the dominant liberal culture. But rather than linking the grand artery with the center, the Ring reinforces the discontinuity by substituting the military belt with a social frontier. See chapter two of Carl E. Schorske, *Fin-de-Siècle Vienna* (New York, 1979).

13   The model of the Athenian Propylaeia haunted architects in the second half of the eighteenth century. Julien-David Le Roy was the first to propose their rebuilding in his *Ruines des plus beaux monuments de la Grèce* (Paris, 1758). On the other hand, it was in Germany that the first building based on the Propylaeia was erected; the Brandenberg Gate by Carl-Gotthard Langhans (Berlin, 1789–1791). It evinced, with the propylaeia at the Konigsplatz by Leo von Klenze (Munich, designed in 1817; realized in 1846–1860), this monumental tradition upon which Loos's work rested.

14   This photomontage was done in 1950 by Ludwig Münz, Loos's friend and partner.

15   A significant resemblance exists between Loos's typologies and those of "neo-rationalist" architects, such as Giorgio Grassi and Aldo Rossi—or Leon Krier, who speaks about the "reconstruction of the European town" (Leon Krier and coll., *Architecture rationnelle* [Brussels, 1978]). Without going into a study of these architects' discussions and their roles as descendants of those such as J.N.L. Durand or Otto Wagner (ibid., pp. 36–37), we can presume their relation, even indirect or unavowed, with Loos and his masters.

16   A. Loos, "The Chicago Tribune Column," *Die potemkinsche Stadt*, op. cit., p. 195.

17   Ibid., p. 196.

18   O. Boissiere, "Le concours du Chicago Tribune revisité," *L'Architecture d'aujourd'hui*, no. 221 (1980), p. 7.

19   *The International Competition for a New Administration Building for the Chicago Tribune*, 1923. See plates 1, 90, 158, 160, 162, 165, 196, and 197.

20   P. H. Scholfield, *The Theory of Proportion in Architecture* (Cambridge, 1958), pp. 50–51 and R. Wittkower, *Architectural Principles in the Age of Humanism* (1949) (London, 1973), pp. 153–154; and further, P. Collins, "The origins of graph paper as an influence on architectural design," *Journal of the Society of Architectural Historians*, vol. XXI, 4 (1962), pp. 159–162.

21   A. Loos, "Projet pour le sauvetage d'une pinède," *L'Architecture d'aujourd'hui*, no. 7 (1931), p. 67.

22   Ibid.

23   It must certainly be the well-known article by Emil Kaufmann, "Architektonische Entwürfe aus der Zeit der französische Revolution," *Zeitschrift für bildende Kunst 63* (May 1929), pp. 38–46.

24   Y. Kurt Unger, "Meine Lehre bei Adolf Loos," *Bauwelt* 42 (November 6, 1981), p. 1891. According to testimony by Unger, it was the gateway reproduced by Emil Kaufmann in his book of 1933, *Von Ledoux bis Le Corbusier*, p. 28.

25   Loos asserted in 1924: "Since the beginning, I have stifled my rage at the movement to reform our ways of teaching design. But man seems to be returning to reason: see, for example, classicism in France. It is now time to speak out." ("Ornement e éducation [1924])," in *Malgré tout*, op. cit. p. 286). Loos defended, in his text, the value of the classical spirit ("an architect is a mason who has learned Latin"), while denouncing "the modern architects who seem more attached to Esperanto" (ibid., p. 290). This position was interpreted as an homage to August Perret (see Nikolaus Pevsner, "Introduction," in L. Münz, G. Kunstler, *Adolf Loos: Pioneer of Modern Architecture*, op. cit.). On one hand, the works of these two architects tended toward the same modern classicism (see M. Tafuri, F. Dal Co. *Architettura contemporanea*, op. cit., Chapter 7); on the other hand, Perret constituted in Loos's eyes, the principle representative of good French architecture. He told young architects looking for work that they could learn esperanto from Le Corbusier, but if they wanted to learn French, they would have to go to Perret (see B. Podrecca, "La même inégalité pour tous," *Adolf Loos 1870–1933*, op. cit., p. 112).

Chapter Seven

1   A. Loos, "Vernacular Art (1914)," in *The Architecture of Adolf Loos*, op. cit., p. 111.

2   A. Loos, "Furniture for Sitting (June 19, 1898)," in *Spoken into the Void*, op. cit., p. 29.

3   Ibid.

4   Roland Schachel, "Adolf Loos, l'Amérique et l'Antiquité," *Adolf Loos 1879–1933*, op. cit., pp. 33–38. According to Schachel, Loos, Semper and Wagner had the same idea of beauty as Socrates (translated from French): "Socrates said of houses, as did Xénophon, that beauty and usefulness must coincide. I see this as an indication of the way in which one should build a house. Basically, the most comfortable and the most beautiful habitat must be one in which one can find, no matter what the season, comfortable refuge and well being." (Xenophone, *Mémoires*, III, 8; cited by R. Schachel, ibid., p. 37). In an analogous perspective, Loos ought to have been able to take into account the dialogue between Socrates and the gunsmith, Pistias (Xenophon, *Mémoires*, III, 10); he gave, however, a version adapted to his time in his didactic history, "Le maître sellier" (*Malgré tout*, op. cit., pp. 154–155).

5   "The English...are our Greeks. It is from them that we acquire our culture; from them that it spreads over the entire globe. The are the consummate men of the nineteenth century." A. Loos, "Glass and Clay (June 26, 1898)," in *Spoken into the Void*, op. cit. pp. 35–36.

6   The four notions of architectural analysis that are developed in this chapter are taken from Paul Frankl, *Die Entwicklungsphasen der neuren Baukunst* (Leipzig and Berlin), 1914. Our interpretation of Loos's work is inspired by the research of German-speaking art and architectural theoreticians who accorded, at the beginning of the century, a particular importance to questions of volume and the perception of image. See Michael Podro, *The Critical Historians of Art* (New Haven and London, 1982); Paul Zucker, "The Paradox of Architectural Theories at the Beginning of the 'Modern Movement,'" *Journal of the Society of Architectural Historians*, vol. X, 3 (October 1951).

7   A. Loos, "Vernacular Art (1914)," op. cit., p. 113.

8   K. Kraus, *Die Fackel*, no. 389–390 (Vienna, December 1913).

Chapter Eight

1   Aldo Rossi, Reyner Banham, Hubert Damisch, Joseph Rykwert, etc.

2   B. Rucschcio, R. Schachel, *Adolf Loos, Leben und Werk* (Salzburg and Vienna, 1982) ; B. Gravagnuolo, *Adolf Loos: Theory and Works* (Milan, 1982).

3   N. Pevsner, *Pioneers of the Modern Movement from William Morris to Walter Gropius* (London, 1936); J.M. Richards, *An Introduction to Modern Architecture* (Harmondsworth, 1940); B. Zevi, *Storia dell'architettura moderna* (Milan, 1950); P. Francastel, *Art et technique, la genèse des formes modernes*

aux XIXe et XXe siècles (Paris, 1956); H.-R. Hitchcock, *Architecture, 19th and 20th Century* (Harmondsworth, 1958); M. Ragon, *Le Livre de l'architecture moderne* (Paris, 1958); L. Benevolo, *Storia dell' architettura moderna* (Bari, 1960).

4   E. Rogers, "L'actualité d'Adolf Loos" and A. Rossi, "Adolf Loos 1879–1933," *Casabella-Continuità*, no. 233 (1959); R. Banham, *Theory and Design in the First Machine Age* (London, 1960); J. Rykwert, "Adolf Loos: the new vision," *Studio International*, no 957 (1973); M. Tafuri, F. Dal Co, *Architettura contemporanea* (Milan, 1976); C. Jencks, *The Language of Post-Modern Architecture* (London, 1977); K. Frampton, *A Critical History of Modern Architecture* (London, 1980).

5   "In his emphasis on monuments and antiquity, Loos is nevertheless perhaps the first to speak of tradition in a modern sense; and he speaks of it as a man of the city, one who knows its old places and houses as if they were family photographs, one who loves old things and their ruin, who knows how each place is steeped in personal history and sees with sadness how all of this is destined to perish.... Only today are we fully able to understand these words, having seen cities and countrysides destroyed by the "system" and by modern architecture's complaisant victory. But modern architecture is an architecture already grown old, beginning with the districts of Frankfurt and any *ville radieuse*; its polemic has by now almost faded away in the wreckage of its own destruction. Meanwhile others, using similar arguments, are now trying to turn the old city or its few remaining fragments into a museum." A. Rossi, "Introduction," in *Spoken into the Void: Collected Essays 1897–1900*, op. cit., p. xi.

6   Ludwig Münz had organized an archive of Loos's works—plans, original drawings, sketches, photos, and models—in preparation for compiling an exhaustive monograph with Heinrich Kulka. But Kulka did not return to Vienna after the war, and Münz died before completing the book.

7   There have been numerous exhibitions of Loos's work, several of which have spawned catalogs: *Das Werk des Architekt Adolf Loos* (Frankfurt, 1931); *Adolf Loos, Walter Gropius* (Bâle, 1931); *Ausstellung Adolf Loos, Bauten und Bildnisse 1870–1933* (Vienna, 1933); *Exhibition of the Work of Adolf Loos at the Architectural Association* (London, 1934); *Adolf Loos* (Tel Aviv, 1947); *Adolf Loos, Mensch und Raum* (Darmstadt, 1951); *Adolf Loos* (Vienna, 1961); *Adolf Loos* (Paris, 1962); *Adolf Loos* (Vienna, 1964); *Adolf Loos* (Rome, 1965); *Adolf Loos 1870–1933* (Zurich, 1965); *Loos Adolf, Wystawa* (Warsaw, 1967); *Adolf Loos für junge Leute* (Vienna, 1970); *Adolf Loos und Josef Hoffmann zum 100 Geburstag* (Vienna, 1971); *Gottfried Semper, Otto Wagner und Adolf Loos* (Vienna, 1977); *Adolf Loos* (Munich, 1982); *Adolf Loos, 1870–1933* (Paris, 1983); *Adolf Loos* (Berlin, 1983–1984); *Adolf Loos* (London, 1985); and *Adolf Loos* (Vienna, 1989–1990).

EXISTING BUILDINGS

Austria

"American Bar"
Kärntner Durchgang 10, Vienna I
1908
Facade partially modified
Building landmarked in 1959

Looshaus (Goldman & Salatsch building)
Michaelerplatz 3, Vienna I
1909–1911
Interior partially modified
Building landmarked in 1947

Knize & Co. clothing store
Graben 13, Vienna I
1910–1913
Building landmarked in 1972

Manz bookshop
Kohlmarkt 16, Vienna I
1912
Building landmarked in 1972

P. C. Leschka & Co. men's clothing store (now a hair salon)
Spiegelgasse 13, Vienna I
1923
Facade restored
Building landmarked in 1972

Anglo-Österreichische Bank (now Zentralsparkasse und Kommerzialbank)
Mariahilferstrasse 70, Vienna VII
1914
Restored
Building landmarked in 1973

Steiner House
St. Veitgasse 10, Vienna XIII
1910
Partially modified

Horner House
Nothargasse 3, Vienna XIII
1912
Partially modified
Building landmarked in 1972

Scheu House
Larochegasse 3, Vienna XIII
1912–1913
Restored
Building landmarked in 1971

Rufer House
Schliessmanngasse 11, Vienna XIII
1922
Building landmarked in 1949

Austrian Werkbund Workers' Housing
Werkbundsiedlung, Woinovichgasse 13, 15, 17, 19, Vienna XII
1930–1932
Buildings landmarked

Moller House
Starkfriedgasse 19, Vienna XVIII
1927–1928
Building landmarked in 1949

Khuner House (now a hotel and restaurant)
Kreuzberg, near Payerbach
1929–1930
Building landmarked

Czechoslovakia

Villa Müller
Stresovicka 820, Prague XVIII
1928–1930
Partially modified

Villa Winternitz
Na Cihlarce 10, Prague-Smichov
1931–1932
Partially modified

House of the Director of the Rohrbach Sugar Refinery
Rohrbach (now Hrysovany), near Brno
1918
Partially modified

France

Tzara House
15 Avenue Junot, Paris XVIIIe
1925–1926
Interior and court elevation modified

Switzerland

Villa Karma
Clarens, near Montreux
1903–1906
Building landmarked

ILLUSTRATION CREDITS

L'Architecture d'aujourd'hui
147.

Der Architekt
133.

Buffotot
32.

Czech, H. and Mistelbauer, W., *Das Looshaus* (Vienna, 1976)
102, 105, 115.

Fischer von Erlach, J. B., *Entwurfe einer historischer Architektur* (Vienna, 1723)
12.

Gerlach photo-studio
7, 16, 18, 19, 21, 22, 23, 25, 28, 31, 39, 57, 62, 64, 66, 74, 75, 77,
78, 79b, 81a, 81b, 82, 94, 97, 98, 106, 117, 126, 127.

Glück, Franz
61, 69b, 95.

Graphische Sammlung Albertina, Adolf Loos Archive
8, 11, 53, 84, 85, 86, 87, 89, 90, 99, 123, 124, 125, 129, 130, 131b,
134, 137, 138, 139, 140, 142, 144, 149.

Historisches Museum der Stadt Wien
5, 6, 100, 101, 103, 104.

Das Interieur
26.

The International Competition for a New Administration Building for the Chicago Tribune (Chicago, 1923)
141.

Kulka, H., *Adolf Loos* (Vienna, 1931)
65, 68, 69a, 70, 71, 72, 73, 79a, 80, 91, 93, 96, 121, 131, 143, 145,
146, 148, 150.

Kunst
17.

Kunstbibliothek, Berlin
3.

Münz, L., Künstler, G., *Der Architekt Adolf Loos* (Vienna, 1964)
83, 92, 136.

Osterkorn
38, 41.

Plan- und Schriftenkammer des Magistrats der Stadt Wien
76.

Podrecca, B. (*A. M. C.* 3, 1984)
54.

Reiffenstein Photo
20, 24, 33, 42, 43, 60.

Rukschcio, B., Schachel, R., *Adolf Loos* (Vienna and Salzburg, 1982)
14, 15, 27, 35, 40, 44, 58, 122, 128.

Schezen, R.
118.

Schinkel, K. F., *Sammlung architektonischer Entwürfe* (Berlin, 1933)
13.

Schlemmer, Jean
56.

Semper, G., *Der Stil* (Munich, 1863)
10.

Surwillo, J.
113.

Tournikiotis, P.
30, 34, 45, 46, 47, 48, 49, 50, 51, 52, 59, 63, 67, 88, 107, 108, 109, 110, 111, 112, 119, 120, 132, 135.

Weiner Sezession, Vienna
4.

Worbs, D.
29.

INDEX

Figures in italics refer to illustration number.